Think GROSS MARGIN!

Bill

GROSS MARGIN

26 Factors Affecting
Your Bottom Line

BILL LEE

GROSS MARGIN

26 Factors Affecting
Your Bottom Line

New Oxford Publishing Corporation
2002

This book was designed to provide accurate and authoritative information in regard to the subject matter covered. It is sold with the understanding that neither the publisher nor the author is engaged in rendering legal or accounting advice. If legal or accounting advice is required, the services of a competent attorney or CPA should be sought.

Senior Editor: Hilary Kanter
Interior Design: Hilary Kanter
Cover Design: Foster & Foster
Printer: Dickinson Press

Library of Congress Cataloging in Publication Data

Lee, Bill

GROSS MARGIN: 26 Factors Affecting Your
Bottom Line / Bill Lee
ISBN 0-9723165-0-7

Printed in the United States of America

DEDICATION

To Clarence B. Bauknight, my mentor and boss for nearly 20 years, for teaching me the rules of business. Without his instruction, inspiration, and motivation, the success I have enjoyed would not have been possible. Clarence got far more productivity out of me than I could ever have gotten out of myself. He is the best businessman I have ever known.

CONTENTS

PREFACE

Gross margin control is really attitude.

An attitude that can best be summed up by a retail owner or manager who has come to realize that the "category killers" of their respective industry have taken an incredible amount of the gross profit margin out of the retail business. By category killers, I'm referring to Wal-Mart, Sam's Club, The Home Depot, Menard's, Best Buy, Circuit City, Target, Lowe's, and dozens of other giant discount merchants that have invaded just about every community in North America.

This book deals primarily with tactics and techniques retailers can use to maintain an acceptable gross margin while remaining competitive. This is, of course, no easy task. "Category killers" use loss leaders and other lowball pricing tactics as their stock in trade. They almost always buy better than their smaller competitors. They are masters at both merchandising and advertising. They're open seven days a week — some of them 24 hours a day. But mainly, their big, bold stores — as large as 175,000 square feet — make a statement that few independent retailers can match.

So to compete, smaller retailers have no choice but to become experts at gross margin control. I believe that not just the owners and managers, but all retail employees who come in contact with a customer can influence gross margin — if they've been taught how.

I've been teaching techniques to increase gross margin

for more than 30 years as a salesperson servicing my customer base, in sales and management seminars that I conduct, and when I've been involved in consulting assignments. The reason for this book, however, is that I've found that retail employees need more than one training session or one workshop; they need a reference manual they can pull off the shelf and review anytime they wish to improve their skill level at optimizing gross margins. To become completely schooled in gross margin control, they need to read and reread key chapters that pertain to their particular role in the retail store.

Some of the factors in this book will apply to retail salespeople. Others will apply to buyers, managers, and road salespeople. So when a retail employee receives a new job with changed responsibilities, he or she needs to become familiar with a completely different set of factors. I believe this book will help serve this need.

GROSS MARGIN CONTROL STARTS AT THE TOP

Gross margin control is not easy. There are no simple answers. It takes hard work on the part of all employees in the business, but gross margins rarely increase in any business unless the owners and other top management personnel are fully committed to enhancing the company's gross margin. Owners, managers, purchasing personnel, and salespeople must become practically obsessed with gross margin enhancement if it is going to happen in your business. But it can be done. I have many clients who very successfully compete against the discounters and still earn a satisfactory gross margin. You and your business can do it, too. So let's get started.

FOREWORD

My interest in the factors affecting gross profit margin began to develop back in 1969, the year I joined Builder Marts of America, Inc. (the name has now been shortened to BMA, Inc.). Several national competitors were putting the fear of God into smaller independent building supply dealers with their massive buying power and superior merchandising techniques. Teaching our customers how to both control gross margin and remain competitive was one of our most valuable value-added services.

In 1976, BMA gave me the opportunity to conduct educational seminars for our retail customer base. Gross profit margin was then, as it is today, a major challenge for just about all business owners, managers, and salespeople. It was a business topic that our customers always wanted to discuss and learn more about.

Before I joined BMA, I had been like a lot of managers: I believed that buying better and figuring out how to raise sell prices were just about the only two ways to improve gross margin. But I was fortunate to have a mentor — a professional manager who was much older and more experienced than I was. Although he was never my direct supervisor, he served with me on BMA's executive committee and had a significant influence on my development as both a manager and an educator. His name was Wade Hampton Stephens. Wade died in 1981, but the lessons he taught me live on and have had a profound impact on my life as a consultant, seminar leader, and writer.

Wade used to describe gross margin as a moving target, something that managers had difficulty getting their arms around. One analogy Wade used to make this point was to say that getting a handle on gross margin was a lot like trying to hold mercury in your hand: When you thought you had it under control, it would slip out of your grasp. Wade taught me that gross margin must be massaged daily, a lesson that still holds true; even with today's sophisticated retail-oriented computer systems, there is no automatic system a manager can put into place to guarantee that gross margin goals will be achieved. I quickly learned that gross margin control was every retail employee's job.

I gained more insight into the factors affecting gross margin control in 1982, the year I began a five-year tour of duty with Enterprise Computer Systems, Inc., a subsidiary corporation BMA had founded in 1976. Enterprise wrote software and sold turnkey computer systems to retailers. We developed the first point-of-sale computer system for the retail building supply industry.

In those days, computer systems were a great deal more expensive than they are today. I remember that back in 1983, our average sale was around $120,000. So in order to sell business owners on investing that kind of money on a computer system, we had to supply some pretty solid evidence that the information the system generated would produce enough additional cash flow to provide a satisfactory return on investment. Gross margin enhancement was high on the list.

In fact, we assured customers that they could improve their gross margins by a full two percentage points if they would abandon their manual systems, install our computer system, and use some of the same gross margin-enhancing techniques that are outlined in this book.

In 1987, I sold my interest in BMA and founded Lee Resources, Inc., a consulting, training, and publishing firm whose mission is to help our client companies improve organizational productivity. Again, gross margin control became a key part of this process. It was at Lee Resources that I had an opportunity to spend countless hours involved in the workings of retail businesses throughout the United States and Canada and was able to finalize the list of factors that this book is all about.

I hope that you and each of your key managers and salespeople will become so familiar with each of the 26 factors that they become almost second nature to you. In the back of the book, on page 172, you'll see a toll-free number to call to order a large poster containing each factor. I recommend that you display this poster on the wall in a private area of the business. Each factor is important. Each plays a part in your company's ability to effectively compete against stiff competition and still earn a satisfactory profit.

Of all the companies I have researched in preparation for writing this book, The Home Depot stands out as a champion of gross margin control. Home Depot's 2001 Annual Report provides a recent history of the company's gross profit margin.

1986 — 27.5%	1994 — 29.9%
1987 — 27.8%	1995 — 27.7%
1988 — 27.0%	1996 — 27.8%
1989 — 27.8%	1997 — 28.5%
1990 — 27.9%	1998 — 29.2%
1991 — 28.1%	1999 — 29.7%
1992 — 27.6%	2000 — 29.9%
1993 — 27.7%	2001 — 31.2%

Factor #1
BUYING BETTER

This chapter will help you understand the impact buying better has on gross margin. You may be surprised to learn, however, that merely buying better is no guarantee that gross margins will increase.

I have listed buying better first, not because it's the most important factor, but because it's the factor most business owners and managers turn to first. Based on my experience with hundreds of clients over the years, I'd say it's probably the one that owners and managers almost always emphasize the most.

One of the reasons I believe this to be the case is because most business owners and executives enjoy buying. Having "checkbook power" is ego boosting. When dealing with a salesperson, buyers have the power to say, "Yes, go ahead and ship it."

But you also have the power to say, "No, your price is out of line. If you want to do business with us, you'll have to sharpen your pencil a little bit."

Anyone who is able to make purchasing decisions has an opportunity to use various negotiating tactics like the one I just mentioned — which can be a lot of fun, especially when they work. This is the reason I believe the buying function is one of the last duties many business owners are willing to delegate — because it is so much fun.

When I speak about buying, I'm speaking from quite a bit of experience. For eight years I headed up purchasing at BMA. At that time, we were the largest buyers in the nation of many so-called commodity building products, so I had a lot of buying power to work with. Any highly competitive person enjoys playing the negotiating game. And I was plenty competitive.

However, buying better by itself won't necessarily have a positive impact on your company's gross margin. In fact, sometimes buying better can even be a detriment to the gross profit dollars your company is able to generate, because so often those responsible for setting sell prices make the mistake of passing on lower costs to the customer. So buying better is an effective gross margin enhancer as long as you're able to continue to sell at prices at least as high as you were selling at before you lowered your cost.

To buy as well as you possibly can, it's important to really study negotiating strategies and tactics. Negotiating is both an art and a science. And like anything, the more knowledge you can gain and the better you can implement that knowledge, the more effective you'll be at improving your company's buying programs.

On pp. 163-165, I have listed several of my favorite books that have greatly improved my negotiating skills. If you want to buy better, read as many of them as you possibly can. The following negotiating tactics, however, are my favorites and have served me well:

1. Do your homework.

One particular year while I was heading up purchasing for my company, we were going through an extremely difficult time getting enough product to satisfy our customers' needs. Demand exceeded supply so much that the manufacturers of one particular commodity product had made the decision to put their products on allocation. This meant that we were allocated just so much product each month and no more.

Allocation is a nightmare for many reasons, but especially when it comes to improving buying programs. In fact, since manufacturers can sell all the product they can make, periods of allocation are usually opportunities for manufacturers to raise list prices outright or reduce competitive discounts that have worked their way into the marketplace.

Our company qualified for a corporate discount, but the manufacturer's sales representative assigned to our account told us the discount was going to be reduced. The manufacturer asked for a high-level meeting between our executives and theirs. They made no secret about it: They were coming for just one purpose — to discuss pricing in general and our corporate discount in particular.

We practically pulled our hair out trying to think of some innovative way to hold onto our corporate discount, but we were getting nowhere. As a last resort, we decided to hire a nationally recognized consultant who had the reputation of being one of the best negotiators, not just in the nation, but in the world.

We set up a conference call. The company's five officers huddled around the speaker phone.

The consultant (I'll call him John) began asking us a lot of questions. We had answers to many of John's questions, but there were many others that we had never even considered. We were about to get a valuable lesson in how to do homework in preparation for a negotiation.

John immediately called the manufacturer's shareholder relations department and ordered a copy of their annual report and their 10-K. That was his part, to scrutinize these reports and find information — any information — that would give us a negotiating advantage.

Next, John assigned each of us four or five questions we were supposed to get answers to. We weren't sure precisely why John wanted some of this information, but we patiently went along with whatever he asked. Several million dollars was at stake. The following are just two of the 20-some apparently unrelated questions John wanted answered:

Q1. What was the manufacturing capacity of the manufacturer's Indianapolis plant?

Q2. What were the details of the senior vice president's bonus plan?

Now you might be thinking that these are some pretty classified pieces of information. And you're right; our supplier never would have volunteered such information had we asked the questions in the course of a formal negotiation. But John gave us a quick lesson on how to extract the answers to these questions from our negotiating partners without raising their defenses. This information became invaluable when the hard bargaining began.

We had explained to John that the members of this particular manufacturer's negotiating team were avid golfers. So anytime we got together — for whatever purpose — a few rounds of golf were arranged if time and weather permitted.

"Be cool," John said as he began. "Don't spook them by asking more than one question over a five- or six-hour period. But when you believe one of [the members of the manufacturer's negotiating team] is relaxed and not expecting anything serious, pop one of the questions in a matter-of-fact sort of way."

My first opportunity came when my golfing partner and I were driving down the fairway together and a few drops of rain fell. Then the rain really began to pour. Since there was no lightning, we decided to seek shelter under a large clump of trees on one side of the course, while the other members of our foursome ducked into a restroom on the other side of the course, out of voice range. We were stuck there, just the two of us, and I thought the time was just about perfect to ask my first question.

"Joe [not his real name], there's something we've been working on that I've been wanting to ask you about. We're in the process of restructuring our officers' compensation plans [which was completely true], and I need some fresh ideas. I got to thinking, you and I have similar responsibilities with our respective companies. If you don't mind my asking, would you give me some idea how your bonus plan is set up?"

Bingo. He willingly told me everything I needed to know. And better yet, he never smelled a rat.

Just as soon as I got back to my hotel room, I quickly made a few notes to make sure I didn't forget any of the details.

As it turned out, another member of our team was across the fairway asking his first question of his golfing partner, a regional vice president:

"Tom, I had an opportunity to go on a tour of that new plant you guys recently built up in Indianapolis. Now that's what I call a state-of-the-art production facility. I've never seen so many sophisticated pieces of equipment. What's the capacity of that plant, anyway?"

Bingo again. Just like that, we had two vital pieces of information that were key to our negotiating strategy.

Each evening, when my three partners and I were together in our hotel room, we would discuss the day's accomplishments and make copious notes of the information and data we'd collected. Then we'd plan what tactics we'd use the next day to get even more of our questions answered.

As it turned out, John wanted to know the details of the executives' bonus plan because, if it became necessary, he would be in a better position to design a strategy that would threaten the amount of bonus the executives would receive. John's theory was that most people become pretty selfish when they're making management decisions that affect their bonus.

He wanted to know the capacity of the Indianapolis plant because he was aware of the importance of incremental profits to a manufacturing company. Since we were relatively naive about cost accounting principles as they apply to the manufacturing process, we had never considered such a tactic.

John made us realize that if we were to convert our business from the Indianapolis plant to a competitive manufacturer, it would have cost our existing supplier approximately 28% of sales in incremental profits — an amount that exceeded the amount of additional profits they would generate by reducing our corporate discount.

By suggesting this option, we brought them to their knees. We kept every dime of our corporate discount.

2. Negotiate higher discounts as your company reaches higher volume plateaus.

My boss for many years, Clarence B. Bauknight, was and still is the best negotiator I have ever known. He is the man who taught me about 90% of what I know about negotiating, including this particular tactic. It's especially effective if your company plans fairly rapid growth. Here's the way it works:

Negotiate the very best deal you can with a supplier, but before you shake hands to finalize the deal, ask your negotiating partner what kind of volume he or she would be happy with in the first 12 months you do business together.

To illustrate my point, let's assume the supplier would be elated if your company purchased $200,000 over the ensuing 12-month period. Try this: Explain to the supplier that you want to go back to your managers, salespeople, and others whose bonus is tied to profits, and offer them an incentive plan that would really get their attention. Ask what kind of additional discount the supplier could justify if your company were able to achieve, not $200,000, but $250,000 over a 12-month period. What about $300,000? $350,000? $400,000? $450,000? $500,000?

In most instances, the supplier won't believe that you can possibly achieve these incrementally higher volume levels, and will agree to additional incentives. As you negotiate, do your best to convince the manufacturer or supplier to leave this kind of multi-tiered discount schedule open-ended. This is critical because if you are on a fast track, you'll hit them a lot faster than you think.

Another good idea: Ask the supplier to pay your company these additional incentive payments in separate checks. This slight procedural adjustment will often internally separate the additional incentive payments from your "standard" discount. Although this is a minor point, it will help you avoid running up a red flag among the supplier's management team. In some instances, we were able to collect these special incentive checks for several years before we were required to renegotiate the original incentive arrangement.

Factor #2
THE MARK-UP RUT

I grew up in Dallas. You're probably thinking that I'm a native Texan, but the Dallas I grew up in was not Dallas, Texas, but Dallas, Georgia. When I was a kid, Dallas was a very small community in northwest Georgia, an hour's drive from Atlanta on two-lane roads that wove through about a half dozen small communities. Today, however, Dallas is practically a bedroom community to the sprawling city of Atlanta.

My father was the managing partner of the local hardware store, Lee Hardware Co. His father and two uncles founded the business in 1894, so he was the second generation to operate the business. Back in the 1940s and 1950s, the store had very little competition because the community simply could not support very many businesses selling hardware, plumbing and electrical supplies, and building materials. Of course, with today's highly competitive environment, these kinds of business environments are few and far between.

One of my most vivid memories of my father's business was our little red "mark-up book." We referred to it often, especially when pricing items we did not stock and had to special order for a customer. Just about every business had one back in those days. I believe we got ours from Beck & Gregg Hardware, an Atlanta-based hardware wholesaler.

As I remember, it contained a page for every mark-up percentage from 1% to 100%.

In the mark-up book, if my memory serves me correctly, there were paper clips marking the 100% page, the 50% page, the 33 $1/_3$% page, and the 25% page for easy reference. And it was one of these four mark-ups that we used for just about everything we sold. I remember that small hardware items like nuts and bolts received a 100% mark-up. In our case, 100% was just about the maximum mark-up we would use.

Of course, higher-volume and more commodity-type building material products like exterior plywood or dimension lumber received a 25% mark-up. As you can see, we were in a classic mark-up rut.

I don't recall that we ever used 200 as a mark-up percentage even on small, insignificant products that were not at all price-sensitive. Nor do I recall trying out 36%, 44%, or 62% mark-ups. We just stuck with what worked for us.

Please don't misunderstand me. My father ran a very successful and profitable business. So even though we were in a mark-up rut, that kind of pricing system was commonplace in that era. But using a mark-up rut as a pricing strategy today is a great way to leave a lot of money on the table.

One way to determine if your company is in a mark-up rut is to look at the mark-ups your people are applying to your product costs. (If your personnel think in terms of gross margins instead of mark-ups, take a look at the gross margins they're using to arrive at selling prices.) How many even numbers do you detect? Too many even numbers are a sure sign of a mark-up rut. Watch for 25%, 33 $1/_3$%, 40%, 50%, 100%. Granted, these are nice round numbers that are easy to remember, but this kind of pricing system usually represents a path of least resistance rather than a solid, well-thought-out pricing strategy.

If you think about pricing logically, however, cost should really have nothing to do with sell price.

Occasionally, my wife, Patti, will be in the middle of

cooking dinner and realize that she's missing an ingredient that's critical to one of the dishes she's preparing. When this happens, she'll usually ask me to drive to the convenience store up the street and pick up the item. Of course, I could drive just a couple of hundred yards farther to the super-market and pay less, but I'm usually in a hurry and figure my time is worth the additional cost.

Since both the convenience store and the supermarket are branches of multibillion-dollar organizations, they probably pay approximately the same amount for the item I'm going to purchase. Yet the difference between the mark-up on cost (and the gross margin each will earn) will be sub-stantially different.

So, you see, a company's cost of goods sold really should have nothing to do with the prices it charges its cus-tomers.

When discussing gross margin control in my seminars, I often ask the audience to take a short "mark-up test." I call out the mark-ups and the audience will tell me the gross margin that each mark-up generates. You may wish to use this exer-cise in your own company with your own employees.

I start with 100%. Almost in unison, the audience will shout 50% gross margin.

"What about 50%?" I ask. "33 $^1/_3$%," they respond.

"33 $^1/_3$%?" They say, "25%."

"And 25%?" "20%," the group answers.

Then comes the question I have the most fun with. "Let's do one more. How much would you have to mark up an item if you want to earn a 75% gross margin?"

Everyone usually smiles sheepishly, looks at each other, but gives no response. Occasionally several members of the audience will take a guess, but it's rare that anyone can come up with the correct answer.

The answer, of course, is 400%. To earn a 75% gross margin, the item must receive a 400% mark-up on cost. *(See Figure 1.)*

Figure 1. Mark-up Required to Achieve
a 75% Gross Margin

Product cost: $48.25   Gross profit: <u>$144.75</u>
Mark-up: 400%   Product sell price: $193.00
Sell price: $193.00
Less cost: $48.25
Gross profit: $144.75

$144.75 ÷ $193.00 = 75% Gross Margin

So if you subtract a cost of $48.25 from a sell price of $193.00, you'll see that on this transaction, we earned gross profit of $144.75. If you divide the gross profit of $144.75 by a sell price of $193.00, you'll see that the gross margin on this sale was 75%.

If employees don't know the formula to earn higher gross margins, they'll usually stick with formulas that they have memorized.

Mathematical Technique

By dividing cost by the inverse of the gross margin you wish to achieve, you will arrive at the sell price necessary to achieve the desired gross margin.

Let's assume that your cost on a product is $1 and you wish to earn a 44% gross margin. The question is: How much must you sell the item for to earn the 44% gross margin. *See Figure 2.*

Figure 2.

To arrive at the inverse, subtract the desired gross margin from 100. In this case, the desired gross margin is 44%, so when 44 is subtracted from 100, the inverse is 56.

A cost of $1 divided by 56 = $1.7857, which we will round to $1.79.

$1.79 sell price less $1.00 cost would equal gross profit of $.79.

Your gross profit of 79 cents divided by a sell price of $1.79 yields a gross margin of 44.13%.

Factor #3
KNOW WHAT THE
MARKET WILL BEAR

I didn't actually see this particular talk show myself, but I heard a story once about a professional sales trainer who appeared on a popular television talk show. After the talk show host and the sales trainer had gone back and forth several times, the talk show host asked the sales trainer this question:

"If you know so much about sales, why don't you show me how you would sell me this ashtray?" referring to an ashtray sitting on his desk.

The sales trainer first asked the talk show host this question: "Well, if you were to buy an ashtray like this one, what do you imagine you could do with it?"

"Oh, I don't know," the talk show host answered. "I don't smoke, but I have several friends who do. I believe it would be attractive and useful sitting on one of the tables outside on my deck."

"Well, if you were to buy an ashtray like this one, what would you envision paying for it?" the sales trainer asked.

"I haven't done a lot of ashtray shopping lately, but I believe it would be worth every bit of $20."

"Sold!" the sales trainer said.

Whether this is a true story or not, I'm not certain, but I do know that it makes an excellent point about what something is worth. Anything that you'll ever try to sell in life is worth no more than what someone is willing to pay for it — in other words, what the market will bear. The market will tell you what your products and services are worth.

So the best way to avoid the mark-up rut I covered in the previous chapter is to analyze the market so carefully that you know what levels of pricing the market will bear. And there's probably only one way to accomplish this — shop the competition.

Sam Walton, modern-day retailing pioneer and founder of Wal-Mart, was famous for scouting out the local merchants to determine where he had to be pricewise in order to achieve the competitive position he was shooting for. "Mr. Sam," as his employees affectionately called him, was both brash and bold. When local merchants spotted him in their retail stores checking out their pricing, he was frequently escorted out the front door. Mr. Sam believed he had no choice; he couldn't merely guess at where his prices needed to be. He felt he must know for sure.

This tactic is still one of the most effective methods for consumer-oriented retailers to determine the prices they must sell at in order to be competitive in the marketplace.

In the building supply industry, the industry leader in the consumer segment of the market is The Home Depot. Founded by Bernie Marcus and Arthur Blank in 1978, Home Depot has become a master of the variable pricing technique. Their use of variable pricing *(see Chapter 15)* has moved the amount the market will bear to new levels in that industry.

Back in 1987 at an industry breakfast in Chicago, I heard a Home Depot executive make the following statement: "We carry 32,000 items in a typical store. On 600 of those sku's, we have the lowest prices in the world. In fact, we defy anyone to beat our prices on any one of them. If competitors attempt to beat our prices, we'll do everything in our power to bury them. But on the other 31,400 items in our store, that's where we achieve our gross margin goals. We may have a low-price image, but just watch us; we're going to make a bunch of money."

Home Depot, the company that claims to have the lowest prices in town, also has been successful at producing one of the highest overall gross profit margins in the retail building supply industry. *(See the chart on page 5.)* For several years, Home Depot's gross margin has hovered in the neighborhood of 29%. On the last annual report I saw, Home Depot's gross margin had risen to 31.2%, and its operating expenses had dropped to under 20% of sales.

In a grocery store, most of us know the price of milk and bread, and maybe even a six-pack of Coke or a pound of ground beef. But when we run out of nutmeg, few of us will shop all over town to find the lowest price; we simply don't have the time, so we toss the container of nutmeg into our grocery cart and never look back.

The so-called discounters have turned the use of loss leaders into a science. They use our human nature against us. They lure consumers into their stores by advertising prices that sound almost too good to be true, thereby fooling the public into believing that everything else is priced at equally low bargain prices.

To counter such tactics, businesses must take time to study the market. They have to actually go out and visit the competition and find out for sure where profit opportunities lay.

If you're in the retail business, shop your competitors frequently. Shop deep into the product assortments they offer. It's important to know what promotions, loss leaders, and special sales the competition is offering to keep from being embarrassed. But to be aware of opportunities to enhance your gross margins, you must shop products that are less price-sensitive. In a grocery store, these items could be spices, black olives, marshmallow cream, or canned artichoke hearts. In an office supply business, you might check paper clips, thumbtacks, or stick-on name badges. In a hardware store, lag bolts, plumbing fittings, or drill bits might be typical.

When one of my Oregon-based clients traveled out of state to shop a competitor that had announced a new store in his market, he told me this: "What shocked me most was not how many prices I had to cut, but how many opportunities we found to raise prices."

OTHER WAYS TO IDENTIFY PROFIT OPPORTUNITIES:

  ♦ Get your hands on the competition's bids or quotations.

  ♦ Ask loyal customers to allow you to take a look at your competitors' invoices.

  ♦ Interview competitors' salespeople who have just been laid off or terminated or who have recently resigned. They will still be familiar with their previous company's pricing structure and will add a great deal to the intelligence you are able to put together.

  ♦ Interview vendor salespeople who also sell your competitors. Ask their advice. If you work hard enough on your relationship with the sales reps who service your account, you'll be surprised at how helpful they'll be at helping you understand your competitors' pricing strategies and tactics.

  ♦ Read your competitors' annual reports. Look for insight into their marketing and pricing strategies.

  ♦ Add your competitors' Web pages to your list of favorite Web sites to visit. You'll be surprised at how much competitive information Web sites contain.

♦ Scrutinize your competitors' print advertising. One effective idea is to prepare a spreadsheet that lists frequently advertised products vertically down the left-hand side of the page. Then list your company's name and the names of each of your competitors across the top of the page. Use a 24-column accounting pad or an electronic spreadsheet to capture this information.

♦ Assign a staff person to go through each competitor's advertising flyers and other advertising material and list the products they are advertising and the price. Be sure to capture the date of the ad and where it ran. This type of research can be invaluable to avoid advertising the identical products. It also gives you solid insight into what the market will bear on price-sensitive items. *(See Figure 3, next page.)*

Figure 3. Let's say that a local retailer is planning an advertising flyer promoting outdoor cooking products. By preparing a chart similar to the one below, the retailer will be in a better position to know more precisely the pricing levels that are being advertised locally:

July 1, 2002
Product, Home Depot

Kingsford Match Light, $9.97

Propane Cylinder Exchange, $16.98

Medallion Gas Grill,
(44,000 BTU), $599

Weber Genesis Silver B
Gas Grill (36,000 BTU), $449

Weber 22.5-in. One-Touch, $79.70

Weber Genesis Silver A
(22,000 BTU), 458 sq. in., $349

Weber 18.5-in. One-Touch, $59.70

Weber 14.5-in. Smokey Joe, $27.84

July 1, 2002
Product, Lowe's

Char-Broil 45,000 BTU Gas, $499

Char-Broil Big Easy Gas
(40,000 BTU) 3 burners, $299

Char-Broil Gas w/side burner,
(35,000 BTU), $159

Char-Broil Big Easy Gas Grill,
(36,000 BTU), $249

Char-Broil 40,000 BTU Gas, $199

Aussie 21 $1/_2$-in. Walk-A-Bout,
332 sq. in., $49.93

Weber 17-in. Smokey Joe,
165 sq. in., $27.70

Thermos Grill 2-Go Gas,
310 sq. in., $148

Factor #4
RAISE PRICES

Anytime you're successful at holding costs constant and raising the prices of your products and services, you'll be able to improve your company's gross margin. Of course, you always run the risk that raising prices will have an adverse effect on sales, but — an impact on sales notwithstanding — it will certainly have a positive impact on gross margin.

Here's one rule of thumb: If your customers are not complaining about your prices, your prices are probably too low. Most business owners and managers are hesitant to raise prices for fear they will lose business. But if you don't try, you'll never know how customers will react. Most businesses don't lose customers over pricing issues. In my experience, far more customers are lost because of poor service than because prices are too high.

It's a better idea to raise prices by small amounts more frequently than to ask customers to accept a mammoth price increase in one fell swoop. So go ahead and test the water. Bump up your prices by a small amount here and a small amount there. In most cases, you'll get only minimal resistance.

Even though cost should have little to do with the price you place on merchandise, your sell prices should be scrutinized each time your suppliers increase their prices. When your prices increase, odds are that your competitors have received a price increase, as well. If you and your competitors must accept a price increase, it's certainly logical that your customers should, too. So don't sit around and wait for the competition to take the lead.

One of my clients is in the convenience store business. He owns about two dozen convenience stores that also sell gasoline. He watches the morning business report on CNN to determine how the price per barrel of oil is fluctuating and uses this information as a guide to set his gasoline prices that day. Rule of thumb: When the oil market is going up, raise prices instantly. But when the price of oil is easing off, drop prices very slowly.

Another excellent time to raise prices is when your business is booming. When I founded my company in 1987, I arbitrarily set my fee for conducting training programs at $1,800 a day. There was only one other person in my industry whom I felt I would be competing with for business; his fee was $1,500 a day and I believed that the information I was sharing with my audiences would be perceived to be of higher value.

After a few months my business began to boom. I was spending far more time traveling than I had ever intended, so I decided to raise my fee to $2,500. I was a bit nervous about the increase, but I decided that I was willing to lose some marginal business in order to establish myself at a higher level.

Not only did my bookings not drop, they were stronger than ever. A year later I increased my fee to $3,000. A year later I raised my fee to $3,600. Each time I raised my fee, my business improved. I finally began to realize that I was a great deal more gun-shy about my fees than my clients and prospects were.

My fee today is $7,100 a day. As a result, we can afford more staff to serve our client base. I have the time to do more research. I also believe that I do much better work since I'm not so tired from so much travel. Now I have the luxury of limiting the number of days I'm on the road.

Looking back on how I set my fee initially, I realize now that I allowed a competitor to influence the value I placed on my services. I was wrong. I should have had more confidence in myself and the value my clients would perceive.

SUPPLY VERSUS DEMAND

When demand exceeds supply, most manufacturers will opt to design some type of allocation plan in an attempt to make sure they don't treat some customers unfairly. But most companies will also use periods of product shortages to inch up prices. After all, you'll certainly have difficulty raising prices when supply exceeds demand. In fact, when there is more product on the market than demand for it, prices almost invariably deteriorate.

Caution: Don't be tempted to gouge your customers when demand exceeds supply. In the late summer of 1992, when Hurricane Andrew devastated many sections of south Florida, literally hundreds of local opportunists flooded the market with essential products, such as generators to provide electricity, roofing products and polyethylene to temporarily replace blown-off roofs, and chain saws. After the area returned to normal, the local population remembered which merchants took advantage of the tragedy and which ones were fair. Always attempt to optimize pricing, but never to the point that your prices will be perceived as "gouging."

Factor #5
SPECIAL-ORDER PRICING

In the course of conducting consulting assignments for retail clients, I interview as many salespeople as I possibly can. I ask dozens of open-ended questions and make copious notes.

To gain insight into how salespeople arrive at the prices they charge for products that must be special ordered, I will typically hold up a photograph of a product I find in an industry trade magazine, one that I feel fairly confident they don't carry in stock.

As I show the salesperson the photograph of the product, I ask the question, "Do you carry this product in stock?"

Assuming they give me a negative answer, my next question is, "If I were to walk into this store and ask for this product, would you special order it for me?"

"Of course, I'd be happy to," would be a typical response.

Then I ask, "Please tell me this: What mark-up or gross margin would you use to arrive at the sell price?"

You would think that I had asked the salesperson to tell me the exact amount of the national debt. The salesperson I'm interviewing will almost always nervously look down at the floor, and then up at the ceiling, and agonize over the answer.

Then about nine times out of ten, the salesperson will

turn to me as if he or she just had a brainstorm and ask, "Do I know you?"

"No, you don't know me," I will answer. "I'm a complete stranger who has walked into your store to buy this item."

But each time I hear this question, I get the distinct impression that if the salesperson did know me, I would be quoted a lower price than if I were a complete stranger.

So since my answer doesn't usually help the salespeople, they will again begin to squirm, acting as if this consultant, a so-called "expert," must know the perfect answer, and they don't. But eventually, they will spit out an answer and say something like, "Oh, I don't know, I guess I'd, er, uh, mark it up 25%."

I write down the answer, neither praise them nor criticize them, and just go on to the next question.

But when I interview the next salesperson, and ask the same question, I get a very similar reaction, and this time around the salesperson may say that the mark-up would be 30%. The next salesperson may say 35%, and so on.

The point is: The odds are slim to none that two salespeople from the same company will say that they would mark up the same item by the same amount. And of course, customers aren't stupid — they eventually figure this out for themselves. After all, they shop the same retail stores, buying the same special-order items month after month. They know which salespeople to avoid (those who have more pricing courage) and which ones to do business with (those who lack pricing courage).

At a business I worked with in eastern Pennsylvania, I interviewed a woman who had been employed at this particular retail store for only about three months. In answer to my mark-up question, she didn't hesitate. She immediately told me that she would mark up the item 58%. A bit shocked, I asked her why she had such a quick answer on the tip of her tongue.

"Well, you see, I came here from a competitor, and at the

competitor's place of business we were given specific mark-ups to apply to each special-order item. For this particular item, the mark-up was 58%. If it worked there, I assumed it would work here. And it does. Ever since I've been working here, my [gross] margins are the highest in the store."

Recommendation: Identify the special-order items that make up 80% of your special-order sales and issue mark-up guidelines to your salespeople or buyers — whoever prices special-order merchandise. Get your salespeople and buyers involved; ask them the mark-ups they believe they can get without losing the sale.

Most customers won't shop all over town for special-order items. They strictly want to place the order and receive it as quickly as possible. They often have a customer they are trying to service, and — at that point — speed of service is a great deal more important than price.

Recommendation: It's also a good idea to consider the dollars of profit on special-order sales and not just the percentage of profit.

Let's say you are special ordering for a customer an item that costs $30. Even if you put a 100% mark-up on that item, you'll earn only $30 in gross profit. At your cost of doing business — writing up the order, calling around to find which vendor can supply it, issuing a purchase order, receiving the merchandise, calling the customer to come in and pick up the item, generating the invoice, and finally collecting for it — the odds are quite good that you'll lose money on that particular order if you earn only $30.

So it's a good idea to determine how many dollars of profit you believe you need to cover your costs and earn a satisfactory profit. Don't rely on mark-up percentages or gross margins alone to arrive at a sell price.

Customer perceptions are critical to the prices your company can command. I believe special-order merchandise represents one of the best opportunities in a retail business to enhance gross margins. If you have a special-order department staffed with courteous, service-oriented, and knowledgeable salespeople who possess excellent product knowledge and a commitment to a fast turnaround, it's almost a guarantee that your customers will be willing to pay a premium for that kind of service.

Remember the old saying: of price, quality, and service, pick any two you wish. It's impractical to expect great service and high quality for the lowest price.

At Sam's Club — the epitome of a successful discounter — most of us expect brand-name merchandise (quality) and low prices, but we don't expect knowledgeable salespeople and high levels of customer service.

Warning: Businesses go broke every day attempting to provide high levels of quality and service at bargain basement prices.

Factor #6
REDUCE RETURNED MERCHANDISE

Returns are murderous to gross margins — and to operating expenses.

Most service-oriented businesses advertise a 100% customer satisfaction policy, meaning that a customer can return just about anything for just about any reason and still receive a full refund. With or without a receipt. Whether the carton has been opened or not. And sometimes (as Nordstrom is famous for) even when the merchandise was purchased from a competitor.

Even when the product is returned in excellent condition, returns are still costly to process. Consider the following costs:

1. In some businesses, picking up the product from the customer.

2. Processing the paperwork at the sales level.

3. Receiving the product back into inventory.

4. Computer input time at the inventory control level.

5. Repackaging the product for possible resale.

6. Returning the product to the manufacturer for credit.

But when the merchandise you're accepting back into inventory is not in a condition to be resold at the full retail price, then returns really begin to eat away at gross margins.

Recommendation: Keep score on returns.

1. What are returns as a percentage of sales?

2. Which customers are primary offenders?

3. Which salespeople are primary offenders?

When you can pinpoint the source of the problem, you'll be in a better position to take corrective action. Businesses frequently do an outstanding job of putting out fires, solving problems, processing returned merchandise, etc. But often they do a horrendous job of preventing the problem in the first place.

If, for example, a customer over-orders and therefore must return the unused portion, what is your policy? I maintain that good customers deserve the benefit of the doubt, but when a particular customer begins to abuse your customer-friendly return policies, it's wise to sit down with that customer and attempt to resolve the problem.

If the customer persists in taking advantage of your return policy — and if you have the pricing flexibility — these additional costs should be reflected in the price you charge that particular customer.

Some salespeople make more mistakes than others. The same is true for operations personnel, such as warehouse workers, material loaders, and delivery personnel. When you're able to isolate key offenders in your own operation, you can also take corrective action. For example, additional training can be a partial solution.

Often, the salesperson doesn't ask the customer enough questions about how the purchase is going to be used. Or worse, he or she has never been taught the right questions to ask. Perhaps the offending salespeople would benefit from spending more time with customers to better understand the application or uses of the products they're selling.

If your business makes deliveries, make sure the merchandise in the warehouse is clearly identified. Color-coded racks and bins often are helpful in reducing shipping errors.

If material you sell is being delivered to a jobsite or other outside storage, you may be able to justify shrink-wrapping the material or sending along plastic sheeting to protect the material from the elements. Then, if the material is returned, odds are that it will be in a more resellable condition.

One of our clients sells a lot millwork, including doors, windows, and lineal mouldings. The delivery personnel were instructed to place the long strips of interior trim in the garage or carport of the home under construction. They found, however, that the construction workers on the job were stepping on and damaging the moulding as they walked through the garage. So when pieces were returned for credit, much of the returned merchandise was dinged and scarred.

During an interdepartmental roundtable session, the group brainstormed the issue of damaged moulding and possible preventive measures. A warehouseman suggested that the warehouse workers use "sawhorse kits" (which the company carried in stock) and make up a supply of sawhorses during the slower winter months. Since sawhorses made from kits break down easily, they would take up very little room on the truck, so delivery personnel could carry them to the jobsite and stack lineal mouldings on top of them. This way, they'd be off the garage floor and less likely to be stepped on. Damage should be minimal.

This is one of the benefits of isolating the specific products that are most frequently being returned for credit. Once problem areas are identified, you've begun to identify a possible solution.

By graphing returns as a percentage of sales, you can get a good idea of the progress you're making. Institute similar routine tracking systems for salespeople and customers.

In a contractor-oriented lumberyard, it's not at all unusual for returns to be as high as 5% of sales. However, by identifying the worst offenders and instituting preventive measures, I've seen that figure drop to less than 2% of sales.

Factor #7
MINIMIZE INVENTORY
SHRINKAGE ("SHRINK")

Inventory "shrink" is a popular term for inventory attrition. And I understand, of course, that some of these 26 factors overlap, just as the impact of returns does with shrink, but shrinkage is such a huge factor that erodes a company's gross margin that it deserves to be discussed by itself and in great detail.

Anytime the value of an inventory item is reduced to the point that you cannot sell it for at least as much as you paid for it, your income statement will suffer from inventory attrition, or "shrink." Here are several examples of "shrink:"

1. Internal or external theft.

2. Write-downs; i.e., when the price of a slow-moving or damaged inventory item must be reduced to below cost to get rid of it.

3. Inaccurate physical counts (undercounts) by inventory-taking personnel at inventory time.

4. More material is loaded on a delivery vehicle than appears on the customer invoice.

5. Material of a higher grade is substituted for material of a lesser grade.

6. A more expensive product is substituted for the product the customer actually ordered. (Service-oriented companies will often substitute when an out-of-stock situation occurs.)

7. Inaccurate and/or sloppy inventory receiving procedures.

Recommendation: Educate employees on the causes of inventory shrink.

When I was in my teens, one of the first jobs my father gave me in his retail store was to participate in the physical inventory-taking process. We always took inventory in January. Like most companies I've worked with over the years, we used inventory teams; that is, one person counted, and the other recorded on paper the quantities that were counted.

This was before the days of computerized inventory, so we had no inventory printouts to make sure we counted everything in stock.

Looking back on those days now, I realize that no one ever explained to us the purpose of counting the inventory items in the first place. And as a result, we were a lot more interested in getting back into the heated store building and out of the unheated warehouses than we were in making accurate counts.

Gross Margin

Here's how I teach it in management seminars, using the cost of goods sold calculation on an income statement or "P&L:"

Sales less cost of goods sold equals gross profit.

Cost of goods sold (COGS) is calculated using the following mathematical process:

Beginning inventory — the dollar value of the inventory we counted last year — plus all of the purchases we've made during the year, minus ending inventory — the dollar value of the inventory we counted this year.

I will use the round figures of a million-dollar business to illustrate:

Sales	+$1,000,000

(Beginning Inventory:	+ $200,000
(Purchases:	+ $800,000
(Ending Inventory:	− $230,000
(Cost of Goods Sold:	$770,000

Cost of Goods Sold	− $770,000
Gross Profit	= $230,000 (23%)

Now let's assume that at inventory time, the people doing the counting were inattentive to detail and produced a less-than-accurate ending inventory. Assume that their accuracy was off by $10,000. So when they turned in their inventory sheets, they understated the quantities that were actually on hand.

Sales $1,000,000

                    (Beginning Inventory: + $200,000
                           (Purchases: + $800,000
                    (Ending Inventory: – $220,000*
                    (Cost of Goods Sold: $780,000

Cost of Goods Sold   – $780,000

Gross Profit   = $220,000 (22%)

denotes where understatement occurred.

In this example, the ending inventory, gross profit, and bottom-line earnings are automatically understated by the same dollar amount.

If the ending inventory were to be *over*stated by $10,000 *(see next page)*, the financial statements would show that the company had actually earned $240,000 in gross profit, and would have paid income taxes on an additional $10,000 in fictitious profits generated purely as a result of a "bad count."

Sales	$1,000,000

(Beginning Inventory: + $200,000
(Purchases: + $800,000
(Ending Inventory: − <u>$240,000</u>
(Cost of Goods Sold: $760,000

Cost of Goods Sold	− $760,000
Gross Profit	= $240,000 (24%)

Recommendation: Take the time to properly train the people who will be involved in the physical counting of your inventory. Make sure they understand the financial consequences of an inaccurate count.

Recommendation: If you are highly conscientious about the accuracy of your physical inventory counts, have one or more employees spot-check behind each inventory team. By recounting key inventory categories, you'll accomplish two things:

1. Your counting teams will be more accurate because they know their counts will be spot-checked.

2. You'll identify the personnel who are less than conscientious; you'll then be able to take appropriate action.

REDUCE SHIPPING AND RECEIVING ERRORS

Anytime customers receive more merchandise than they paid for, shrinkage occurs.

Discount stores often post a "checker" at the front door to double-check the merchandise in the customer's shopping cart against the cash register receipt. Although this procedure certainly reduces shrinkage (by catching both honest and dishonest mistakes), some merchants believe that it sends a bad customer-service message.

Retailers who deliver merchandise to their customers are encouraged to assign an employee with strong product knowledge to double-check the merchandise on the delivery vehicle against the merchandise listed on the invoice or shipping papers. This practice reduces both errors and theft.

Incoming shipments from suppliers must also be checked for accuracy if shrinkage is to be held to a minimum. I recommend assigning specific personnel to "receive" merchandise. It's also wise to specify backup personnel to receive goods if the primary person assigned is unavailable. But I discourage allowing incoming inventory to be received — that is, counted — by just anyone who happens to be available.

Highly conscientious companies often do not give receiving personnel access to the quantities that have been ordered. This is accomplished by asking your forms supplier to black out the quantity column on the copy of the purchase order that the receivers use to receive merchandise.

Since the vendor's shipping papers usually note quantities as well, it's wise to institute a procedure whereby all drivers of supplier delivery vehicles drop off the shipping papers with a designated person before proceeding to the unloading area.

REDUCE THEFT

It takes a team effort to reduce internal and external theft. The first step is to hold team meetings to discuss techniques thieves use to steal merchandise. While shoplifting is common in consumer-oriented retail stores, commercial and industrial customers must also be scrutinized.

I'll never forget a story one of my clients told me that illustrates how clever a dishonest customer can be. This retailer sold paint, primarily to professional painters. One particular painter (we'll call him George) had been a loyal customer for more than ten years. He bought all of his paint from my client, and anytime he had paint left over from a job, he was allowed to return the excess paint for credit.

One day, a paint salesman was standing in one of the rooms of the store where paint was warehoused taking an inventory of the store's various products. He could easily see the dock area behind the store from where he was standing. The salesman saw a pickup truck pull up to the parking area and park next to the stairs. George got out of his truck empty-handed and took a shortcut through the storeroom to get to the showroom. As he walked through the storeroom, George picked up two gallons of oyster white latex wall paint in each hand and proceeded into the store.

The salesman was curious, so he followed George, but not so close that he would be seen. The salesman watched George walk up to the retail counter and place the four cans of interior latex on the counter.

"I need credit on these, Joe, and I need to pick up enough [paint] for the DePolo job."

The salesman told the owner what had happened and the owner began to watch George. After seeing him do this several times, the owner installed two small video cameras over the door so he could capture George's every move as he got out of his truck, picked up paint he had not paid for, and walked to the retail counter. He caught him red-handed. George confessed and settled with the owner for several thousand dollars.

In my opinion, the only mistake the owner made was lacking the courage to prosecute him.

Recommendation: Someone should be assigned to watch

loading areas to which customers have access. When customers drive around to the loading dock to pick up merchandise they've ordered, it's critical to make sure they don't pick up something that doesn't appear on their loading ticket.

When shrinkage persists and management is convinced that internal theft is taking place, retailers will often hire an undercover agent to pose as an employee and attempt to infiltrate the internal theft ring.

Factor #8
ADD-ON SELLING

Suggestive selling and related-item selling are other names retailers give to "add-on selling."

In the consumer portion of today's retail marketplace, the use of loss leaders is the leading marketing tactic that North America's superstores employ to lure consumers into the store. Inside, however, customers are sure to find "islands of losses amid seas of profits." Retailers would go broke selling nothing but advertised specials at cost, near cost, and sometimes below cost. So related-item selling is not only a nice-to-have, it's a got-to-have if you expect to optimize gross margins.

Most related items are not as price-sensitive as the core product, so if the retailer has a sharp pricing system, related items carry significantly higher gross margins than the core product.

In many instances, however, related-item selling is every bit as much a customer service tool as it is a technique to enhance gross margins. As consumers, all of us have at one time or another come home from a trip to a retail store only to realize that we've forgotten an item that's necessary to complete the project we're working on. So salespeople who are trained to remind customers not to overlook an accessory product that goes hand in hand with a core product can save their customers a lot of time while enhancing their company's gross margin.

Paint always comes to mind when I think about related-item selling. Imagine a consumer walking through a retail paint store, drawn to a large sign advertising interior latex paint on sale at a ridiculously low price. Impulsively, the consumer picks up a few gallons to paint a bedroom, a project she has been putting off for months.

But after arriving home, she realizes that she has forgotten several essentials: a paint roller and pan, a drop cloth, and clean-up materials. So, glancing at her watch to see if she still has time to get back to the store before it closes, she jumps back into her car and dashes back to pick up the items she has forgotten. This common scenario could have been avoided if the salesperson had only been trained to ask about related items.

Just about all products in all industries require related items: Computer customers need printer ribbons and cartridges, printer paper, keyboards, diskettes, and software.

Customers visiting a men's store need ties, shirts, handkerchiefs, and belts to accompany the purchase of a suit of clothes.

Customers purchasing a VCR at an electronics store might also be in need of videocassette tapes, a head cleaner, and a videotape rack.

Home center customers purchasing a power drill need drill bits. If they're purchasing a power saw, they need saw blades.

Fast-food restaurants are not very professional in the way they use this gross margin-enhancing technique, but most consumers have at one time or another been a victim to that voice over the speaker that says, "Do you want fries to go along with that cheeseburger?" You may have initially decided to exercise some discipline and forgo French fries today, but that little bit of prompting caused you to answer, "Yeah, go ahead and include fries."

The reason I say that most fast-food restaurants are relatively unprofessional when they use this technique is because they're usually in a hurry and ask customers about related items as if their supervisor is forcing them to do so. The related-item sales technique is most effective when salespeople are properly trained and have practiced using effective and well-rehearsed voice intonation.

When I was purchasing a new printer recently, the salesperson said, as he very professionally picked up my name from my credit card, "Mr. Lee, you made a good choice when you selected this printer. It's a new model that should give you several years of service. There's one thing you should know, however. This printer uses a special toner cartridge that's sometimes hard to find. You may be wise to buy a couple of extras. We have plenty in stock, so if you'd like, I'll be happy to add them to this ticket."

This is an excellent example of how related-item selling can be an excellent customer service tool. First of all, I had not thought about purchasing extra toner cartridges, so I appreciated the salesperson's suggesting that I do so. And second, if, in fact, the cartridges were really as difficult to find as the salesperson suggested, I would have been scrambling all over town looking for them when my new printer did run out.

Product knowledge is essential to related-item selling. If the salespeople don't understand how the end user uses their products, the accessory products, and the tools required, they will not be in a very good position to suggest related items. There are a number of ways salespeople can gain sufficient product knowledge to do an effective job of suggestive selling.

1. Invite the manufacturers' reps or wholesalers' reps who service your account to conduct product knowledge sessions for your buyers and sales staff.

For added benefit, videotape these sessions. That way, you can build a library of training materials for use in training salespeople you hire in the future. If you take me up on this idea, I recommend that you give the supplier as much advance notice as you can so the person doing the training will have adequate time to prepare. Warn the trainer that the session will be videotaped. This advance notice that the program will be taped often qualifies you for a more qualified trainer, such as a sales manager or product specialist.

2. One way to learn is by teaching. At sales meetings or store meetings, invite each of your customer-contact employees to conduct a product presentation. Give them plenty of notice so they will have time to prepare. In the course of the preparation, ask the trainer to include 20 to 25 pertinent questions that will serve as a quiz to test the other employees' understanding of the material presented. If you save these questions by product category, you'll eventually have an excellent product training course for new employees who come on board. Just make sure that one of the questions is to list as many related items as possible.

3. Another excellent way to learn about related items is for sales personnel to spend time with customers, watching them use the products your company sells. Most retailers have loyal customers who would be willing to allow your customer-contact personnel to "look over their shoulder" from time to time. As a part of training programs for new employees, many retailers make deals with several loyal customers to allow the trainee to work with the customer for a predetermined period.

4. Many point-of-sale computer systems are programmed with an option that's frequently referred to as a related-item sales feature. Here's how it works: When the computer software is being set up, there's a screen in the inventory control module that asks the operator to input the related items that are to appear on the screen when that par-

ticular item is entered. So when the system is activated and the retailer is ready to "go live," each time a core product is sold, a related-item message appears at the bottom of the screen that reads: "Ask about the following related items," and the salesperson is alerted to ask the customer about additional products that he or she may need.

5. Try this related-item exercise as a training tool. At sales meetings or store meetings, hand out a list of eight or ten products your company frequently advertises. Leave a dozen or so blanks under each product and give the attendees 15 minutes to list as many related items as they possibly can. Then go around the room and ask each person to name just one related item that he or she has on their list. Ask all attendees to add any item named to their list if they had not already included it. This is a great way for salespeople to keep related items fresh in their minds. At the end of the meeting, collect the lists and ask an assistant to log them into one of the company's PCs. Soon you'll have an excellent list of related items to add to the company's training manual.

Factor #9
SELLING UP

Upgrade sales to higher-quality, premium products.

The rule in most industries is that the more premium the product, the higher gross margin it carries. Remember the old story that used to go around the circuit about a national retailer? As the story goes, the retailer made it a practice of advertising low-quality loss leaders to get consumers into the store, but the salespeople were told that anyone who sold the loss leader — that is, anyone who failed to upgrade the sale — would be fired.

This concept is often called good, better, best.

In years past, I've made the mistake of trying to save money by purchasing low-quality advertised products. But I soon learned that over the long haul, I wasn't really saving money at all; in fact, in my attempt to save, I was spending too much. If I had only paid a little more up front, I would have saved a lot more on the back end.

Today, I seek out salespeople who have enough product knowledge and care enough about me as a customer to spend the extra time necessary to help me purchase products that provide the best value, not necessarily the lowest cost.

How about you? Have you ever wished a salesperson who allowed you to purchase a low-quality product had been just a little bit better trained or had been just a little bit more persuasive? Most of us have.

Again, the better the product knowledge, the better equipped salespeople will be to sell up.

Back in 1965 I bought my first home. One of the first purchases I had to make was a power mower. Since I was making very little money at the time, I was looking for the cheapest power mower I could find. I watched the advertising flyers in the local newspaper and found the least expensive mower at Kmart, priced at $39.95. Wow, I thought, what a deal, so I went down to look it over. The mower had a Briggs & Stratton engine, so I assumed it had to be OK. I bought the mower.

Sure enough, after I put oil and gasoline in it, the engine cranked right up. I was so proud of myself, getting such a bargain. I used the mower all summer.

But the next spring, the mower wouldn't start. I pulled and pulled the starter cord, but nothing happened. So I took the mower into a repair shop and paid $30 to have it fixed. I had trouble with the mower all summer, sometimes wrestling with it for 20 to 30 minutes before it would start. I decided that while $39.95 was certainly a low price, it wasn't necessarily a good buy.

Twenty years and at least a half dozen mowers later, I was again in the market for a new lawn mower. But this time around, someone told me about the virtues of a Honda mower. I looked in the Yellow Pages and found a local Honda dealer. I drove to the dealership and saw the mower sitting out front. It was self-propelled and had a large grass catcher on the rear that was easy to remove and replace. Then I saw the price tag — $400.

I couldn't believe my eyes. "You've got to be kidding," I told the salesperson.

"Sir," the young salesperson said as I turned to look at a less expensive mower, "that mower is expensive, but there's a reason. A Honda is the best lawn mower on the market today. How about taking time to reach down and pull the starter cord?"

So I leaned over and gave it a strong pull. It cranked immediately.

The salesperson killed the engine and said, "You didn't really have to pull the cord that hard, sir. If you don't mind, try it again, but this time, just barely pull the cord."

So I followed his instructions and pulled the cord maybe six inches. It started just as before.

"Now that's the mark of a Honda," he said, and he smiled as if he was really proud of the product he was selling.

"But $400, that's a lot of money," I complained.

"Yes, it is, but think about it this way: It'll probably be the last mower you'll ever have to buy. It'll last for years and years," he said. "About all you'll ever have to do is change the oil and occasionally replace the spark plug. And if you'll bring it in to us, we'll do the annual maintenance for you."

I grimaced as I wrote out the check for $400 plus tax. That was a good 10 years ago, and that Honda mower is running as well today as the day I bought it. I learned a good lesson that I've never forgotten — there's a big difference between price and cost. The price of the Honda was 10 times that of the mower I bought at Kmart, but over the years it actually cost me far less. And when you add the peace of mind and the lack of frustration, I realized that there was no contest between buying the best versus buying the cheapest.

I had the same experience with my first home. The builder was a competent builder, but he wasn't a very good salesperson. He gave me a number of options when we went over the plans, and I selected the least expensive on each. Our home had very little interior trim such as crown moulding, chair rail, etc. The window frames were made of aluminum and had no windowsill at all — again, the cheapest option. The only exception was the roof. At that time, I worked for the Ruberoid Co., an asphalt roofing manufacturer that was later acquired by GAF Corp. I did understand roofing and specified a 300-pound roof that had a 25-year warranty. Granted, I was inconsistent, but I really enjoyed that roof. The reason: I knew it was the best.

When I was transferred 18 months later, the house sat on the market for almost a year before it sold. The reason: Compared with other houses in the same subdivision, my house had the fewest amenities.

Salespeople who are skilled at selling up — that is, helping their customers make quality buying decisions — are doing their customers a huge favor. When you buy quality, you enjoy the purchase much more. When you buy quality, the product lasts longer. And when you buy quality, you almost always pay less in the long run. You don't have to replace the product as often. It's usually less expensive to maintain. And when it's time to sell or trade, the higher-quality product will almost always bring a higher price.

Consumers cannot possibly know as much about the products they buy as the salespeople know about the products they sell. So salespeople who don't help customers make wise buying decisions are doing the customer an injustice.

The up-selling process begins like all selling begins — by asking good, open-ended, probing questions. Here are some examples:

1. How do you plan to use the product?

2. For how long do you plan to use the product?

3. What kind of project are you working on?

4. How important is it for you to minimize the cost of ongoing maintenance?

5. How important is performance?

6. Is your goal to minimize how much you pay or optimize the value you receive?

7. What kind of image are you trying to achieve?

8. How important is resale value?

9. How many times would you typically wear or use this product before cleaning?

10. How much time do you spend using this product?

11. What are your priorities?

12. You've used this product before. What improvements would you like to make this time around?

13. After you begin using this product, how will you evaluate your decision?

14. How important are dependability and consistency?

When I worked for the roofing manufacturer, we made the highest gross margin when we sold premium roofing products. Bear in mind that this was back in the mid-1960s, but at that time, our highest-volume — and lowest gross-margin — product was a 235-lb. asphalt roofing shingle that carried only a 15-year warranty. The most effective question we taught salespeople to ask was, "How long do you plan to live in this house?"

If they answered something like, "We hope this is the last home we ever own" or "for the rest of our lives," we believed we were in a good position to upgrade the customer to a premium shingle. We did this by attempting to prove to the customer that the more expensive product is really less expensive if you think longer-term. You see, if you divide the price you pay for a 30-year roof by 30 (labor expense to install the product is almost identical for both products), you'll come up with a lower annual cost than if you divide the lower-priced product by 15 years.

When my mother-in-law bought a home in the mid-'60s, the builder used the least expensive products he could buy to keep the house in a competitive price range. Over the years, she spent many thousands of dollars replacing these "cheap" products with products of a higher quality. When she was preparing to retire, she invested in a 100% maintenance-free exterior. She knew that on a fixed income, she would not have as much money to spend on maintenance. Vinyl siding was installed over the wood clapboard; vinyl was installed on the fascia and soffits. Her next project is to replace the wood windows with a vinyl-clad product.

Think about how much less this house would have cost her if the builder who built her home had had the foresight to use higher-quality products. The nation's most profitable residential builders have, in fact, developed the sales skill of selling up. They also say that they can sleep a lot better at night knowing they've built a home that will stand up to the test of time.

Factor #10
TEACH SALESPEOPLE
TO DEAL WITH
PRICING OBJECTIONS

I don't know about you, but just about anytime I make a purchase for a large amount of money, I try to get the salesperson to lower the price. Now I don't go so far as to ask a cashier in a grocery store to give me a special deal on a gallon of milk, but when buying a suit, I always ask for a discount. And if that doesn't work, I'll ask if it's possible to throw in a couple of ties at no charge. You'd be surprised at how often the salesperson will comply with my request.

It's not unusual for salespeople to have some pricing flexibility. If the salesperson is compensated on some kind of commission arrangement that's not tied to gross margin, I've found that they will frequently fall for basic negotiating tactics — like the flinch.

The flinch tactic is as old as the hills, but it's highly effective. Here's the way it works: You ask the salesperson the price. Just as soon as he gets the words out of his mouth, the customer practically goes into orbit. "Good grief!" the customer screams. "Get out of here, I didn't ask for a [product name] that was gold plated. You've got to be kidding."

"Well, what if I could get you a 10% discount, would that make you feel any better?" the salesperson might respond.

"Ten percent, you're still sky-high at even a 10% discount, but that's a lot better than that ridiculous price you gave me the first time around."

The first rule in negotiating is to never give away a concession without getting something in return. In the illustration above, the salesperson fell prey to the flinch, lowered his price, and he is not even assured of getting the order.

All salespeople will sooner or later experience the flinch, so it's essential that they learn how to respond without giving away the store. I recommend the reverse flinch. It goes something like this: The salesperson gives the flinching customer a look of disbelief and says: "How do you mean our price is high? Gee whiz, we spend a fortune shopping the market and we're constantly getting a look at competitors' prices. I don't understand. I've had a great week, and just this morning I was talking to my sales manager, and he told me that our entire company had had a record month. Could you give me a little more information?"

Now that's a pretty good reverse flinch, if I do say so myself.

One of the best ways to get a lower price is to ask for a discount. I do it whether I'm buying antiques, wine, or electronics. Again, you'd be surprised just how often the salesperson will say, "Sure, I'm authorized to give a 10% discount." But even if the salesperson says no, it costs nothing to ask.

One of my favorite stories about discounting began when my wife asked me to meet her at a downtown furniture store to "approve" an armoire she had spotted the day before.

But to properly understand the circumstances, you need to know a few more things. For years my wife had been looking for a relatively narrow armoire to fit a rather narrow master bedroom wall between our walk-in closet and our master bath. Up until now, every one she had found was too wide for that particular wall.

Then, finally, she discovered the seemingly perfect armoire at a store right in our own hometown. I have to laugh a little when I tell this story because this was the kind of purchase that she was going to make with or without my "approval," but to keep peace in the family I agreed to join her during my lunch hour.

As my wife and I stood outside the store before going inside, I advised her to be cool. "Don't appear overly enthusiastic about the armoire because I'm going to do my best to get the salesperson to give us a discount. Just let me do the talking," I told her very clearly as we opened the front door and walked inside.

As we entered the store, a young saleswoman greeted us at the door. "May I help you?" she asked. "No, we're just look...," I started to say as I heard my wife loudly exclaim, "Honey, come over here. Is this piece of furniture perfect, or what? And it's the least expensive one I've seen anywhere." My wife was so excited about finding an armoire the right size that she had all of a sudden developed a serious case of amnesia. She had completely forgotten the instructions I had given her before we walked into the store.

Now I knew I had my work cut out for me.

One piece of information that I didn't share is that while shopping the store the day before, my wife had also found a pencil post bed that she felt would be perfect for our daughter's old room, which we were in the process of converting into a guest room. So as we were walking toward the back of the store where the pencil post bed was on display, I asked the saleswoman, "Do you folks discount your prices?"

"Well," she said rather routinely, "I'm not allowed to discount."

"Well, who is?" I asked.

"The manager," she answered.

"And where is the manager?" I asked.

"She's at lunch and won't be back until around 2," she said.

My wife and I walked out of that store without the armoire and without the pencil post bed. When we were on the sidewalk where our negotiating strategy had begun, she made it perfectly clear just what would happen to me if for any reason someone else purchased the only armoire in the world that would fit the narrow wall in our bedroom.

Naturally a bit nervous since my life was practically at stake, I telephoned the furniture store at about 1:45 p.m. Luckily, the manager was back from lunch. I used the following negotiating tactic:

"Ms. McAbee, my wife and I are really excited about the armoire your salesperson showed us in the front of the store. I'm sure we will probably go ahead and buy it, but we also have a casual interest in the pencil post bed in the back of the store. I'm not at all sure we can afford both, but if we were to buy both, would there be a discount?"

"Yes, Mr. Lee," she replied, "If you buy both and if you buy them today, we'll be happy to extend a 15% discount."

"Now, wait a minute, Ms. McAbee, for a purchase of this size I had more in mind a discount of 20%."

"I'm sorry, Mr. Lee, but even if you buy every piece of furniture in the store, 15% is our maximum discount."

"Ms. McAbee, may I ask one more question? Do you accept credit cards?"

"Why, yes, we do. We accept both Visa and MasterCard."

"Well, then, please write down my Visa number and mark that armoire and the pencil post bed SOLD."

Now that you know the entire story, you'll have to admit that I had little choice but to buy the armoire whether I was successful in getting a discount or not. All Ms. McAbee had to do was to say something like, "I don't know, Mr. Lee, that armoire has been a very popular piece of furniture. I'm not sure, but I believe someone may be coming back this afternoon to make a decision on whether to buy it." She could also have said, "Mr. Lee, that armoire is already discounted as much as I can possibly discount it."

If she had come back at me with either response, what do you think my reaction would have been? You're right, I would have bought it immediately. After all, it was the only armoire in the world that would fit that bedroom wall.

The moral of the story is to stand up for your prices. Your company is successful because it offers a good value for the prices it charges. Nine times out of ten, a pleasant rebuff is all that's necessary to make customers feel good about the price they're paying. Most customers just want to make sure they aren't leaving money on the table by not at least asking for a discount.

Dozens of books on effective negotiating are available in the bookstores, and if you'll check with your Chamber of Commerce, most offer seminars on negotiating skills. Negotiating is a game, just like baseball or football. There are basic rules involved.

I tell my seminar audiences that a flinch, for example, is not unlike a head fake in football or basketball. To reduce the odds that I would fall prey to a head fake, my high school coach taught me to keep my eyes on the opponent's hips or belt buckle and to avoid eye contact. This defensive tactic is no guarantee that the head fake won't work, but it certainly reduces its effectiveness.

Another negotiating technique that salespeople frequently experience is when a buyer says something like, "You can do better than that." It's sort of an open-ended statement that almost requires a response. When you hear these words come out of a buyer's mouth, you must recognize them as a clue that the buyer may be using another negotiating technique typically referred to as the krunch.

The krunch often comes in three phases, but it almost always begins with, "You can do better than that." Inexperienced salespeople will typically react to the krunch by exercising whatever pricing authority they have and "do a little better." The next phase of the krunch comes when the buyer says, "You're getting real close."

Now, most salespeople want one thing more than anything else — an order. So when the buyer tells them that they're "real close," overly optimistic salespeople will usually convince themselves that if they come off their price just one more time, they will surely get the order. So they cut the price a little bit more. But no order is forthcoming, because buyers who are skilled at the krunch still have phase three up their sleeves. Phase three is, "You're almost there."

The problem here is that the salesperson who reduces the price twice has already unconsciously told the buyer that he or she has pricing authority. The buyer is just trying to determine where the bottom is. Once again, the salesperson is suckered into reducing the price before the buyer has committed.

The best defense against the krunch is to see it coming and thereby avoid getting snared in the buyer's trap. When I hear the words, "You can do better than that," it's a warning sign to me. My response is something like, "Mr. Buyer, I have given you a really good deal here. You're getting a highly competitive price, and we are going to give you excellent service. Please don't ask me to do more than I can do. I've already given you my best possible price."

The krunch, like the flinch, is usually an attempt on the part of buyers to make sure they are getting the best possible price and aren't leaving money on the table.

If you do begin studying the fine art of negotiating and enhance your skills, you'll find that customers and prospects will quite often try tactics that are more subtle than the flinch or the krunch.

Back in the early 1980s, I was in the computer business. My company, Enterprise Computer Systems, Inc., sold turnkey point-of-sale computer systems. I was a vice president over sales and marketing. We had a sales force that covered the entire United States and occasionally would trek over the border into Canada. It was not unusual for one of our salespeople to be sitting in an owner's or manager's office and have the decision-maker ask a question like this: "Our understanding is that we will have to trash our current business forms if we install your system. Is this the case?"

Our salesperson would answer honestly, "Yes, that's true."

"Will your company extend to us a credit for those forms?" would be a typical next question.

If our salesperson had been trained properly, he or she would ask the decision-maker, "How much money would you estimate we are talking about?"

"Oh, I don't know, but I'd guess we have no less than $5,000 in business forms in our storeroom."

Before I go any further, I should explain that back in those days, the average price we charged for a typical computer system was $120,000. And our gross margin on the average sale was in the neighborhood of 60%. The reason our gross margin was so high was because of the way we handled our cost accounting back then; the software portion of the sale was 100% gross profit. Our gross margin on the hardware portion was around 25%.

So the salesperson, hungry for an order, would often spit out, "Sure, we'd be happy to give you a $5,000 forms credit. Are you ready to configure the system today?"

"No," the decision-maker would say, "We've just begun our search."

It's pretty obvious what the salesperson just did: He or she violated the number one rule in negotiating: *Never give up anything without getting something in return.* The salesperson gave away $5,000 and got nothing in return.

This was happening so often to our young sales force that we instituted a negotiating technique called "resort to higher authority." We taught our salespeople to use a conditional phrase to prevent them from falling into that trap. If the buyer asked for a concession, they would respond with a question: "If I could get my boss to agree to a $5,000 forms credit, would you be willing to sign the sales agreement today?"

If the buyer said yes, then the salesperson had an order. If the buyer said no, then the salesperson could ask, "Then what other issues do we need to discuss?"

Salespeople must remember that when they cut the price, each dollar comes off not only the gross profit line on the financial statement, but off the pretax line as well. Salespeople must be trained to deal with the negotiating tactics buyers use so effectively.

Some customers don't feel they've done a good day's work until they've been able to get a salesperson to lower a price. So whatever price the salesperson quotes, it's never good enough. And this kind of buyer simply will not issue final authorization unless the price is reduced.

Like most sales trainers and consultants, I despise the tactic used by so many automobile dealers — pricing their product at an unrealistically high list price and forcing the buyer to negotiate down from there. It's not that I'm intimidated by the negotiating process — after all, I teach negotiating — it's that I don't have time to learn as much about the car business as the car dealer knows. Since I'm at a disadvantage before we ever begin the haggling process, I refuse to do business with a car dealer who insists on doing business this way. Fortunately, many dealers are beginning to institute a no-hassle, no-negotiating pricing policy. All Saturn dealers and most Lexus dealers have adopted this strategy.

But if you do business with the same customers over and over, you get to know them pretty well. You have the luxury of doing business the way your customers like to do business rather than rigidly doing business only the way you or your company wants to do business.

So when you have customers who simply cannot bring themselves to pay your asking price, you have little choice but to take a page out of the car dealer's book and quote an initial price that's higher than your target price. If, for example, your target price is $443, you might decide to go in at $467. Then when the buyer demands a lower price, you have room to move without jeopardizing your gross margin.

Warning: Before going into a negotiation like the one just described, be sure not only to decide on an initial price and a target price, but also on a walk-away price. The walk-away is the price below which you refuse to go regardless of what the buyer says or does.

In the example above, and assuming that you do have this degree of pricing authority, you might privately agree on the following pricing scheme:

Initial price: $467

Target price: $443

Walk-away price: $439

By deciding on a walk-away, you'll protect yourself from becoming so intoxicated with the prospect of making a sale that you lose your head.

There's a recommended reading list for salespeople on page 164. The books listed will help you become a better negotiator. Many of your customers have already read such books and have attended seminars to improve their negotiating skills, so to play on a level playing field, you must work on your negotiating skills, as well. When you've improved your skills at overcoming pricing objections, your gross margin will be much less vulnerable.

Factor #11
ELIMINATE EMPLOYEE GUILT

I learned this lesson early in life from my father. One day, one of our family's best friends, Mr. Gene Bullock, came walking across the town square in the direction of my dad's store. He approached my dad, made a small purchase, and was quickly on his way.

When my mother moved to Dallas, Georgia, back in 1928, she lived in Mr. Bullock's parents' home as a boarder. We considered the members of the Bullock family to be among our closest friends, so with a child's natural curiosity, I asked my dad, "Did you make a profit on that item Mr. Bullock just bought?"

"Yes, I did, son. Why do you ask?"

"I can't believe you would make a profit on Mr. Bullock. He's one of our best friends. Why wouldn't you just sell him, say, at cost?"

I'll never forget my dad's answer: "Son, if you can't make a profit on your friends, you certainly can't make a profit on your enemies."

My dad made a great point. After all, in the 1940s in Dallas, in a community where most everyone knew everyone else, virtually all of our customers were our friends. But this kind of thinking — to give friends a deal — is still prevalent today.

A couple of years ago, a Midwest client read an article I had written on gross margin control and asked me to come out and speak to his sales staff on the topic. The client had several small retail locations in a rural section of the state. Most of the towns where his retail stores were located had populations of 500 to 1,000.

When I interviewed the owner, he told me that his gross margin had been in a state of steady decline for several years, and that his company had actually lost money for three years in a row. He didn't even ask my fee; he just needed help, and he needed it fast. So we made the arrangements for my visit very quickly, and I was on my way.

After I arrived on site for the seminar, I realized pretty quickly that I was in trouble. I could tell from their body language that the men and women in the audience didn't want to be there. Their arms were folded across their chests, and there was not even the hint of a smile on anyone's face.

For the first time in my career as a seminar leader, I was bombing. Nothing I said or did could get the employees in the audience into a positive, participative mood. So at the first break, I explained to the owners what my feelings were and asked them to leave the room. Maybe, I thought, just maybe, if the owners were not in the room I could get better results.

Wow! The tactic worked like a charm. With the owners out of the room, the audience began to perk up. In fact, one rather outspoken man in the back of the room stood up and took it upon himself to explain the situation to me.

He said that in the small communities where their stores are located, everyone knew everyone else. "You see, Mr. Lee, most of our customers are farmers. If you've been reading the newspapers lately, you realize that the farmers in this region of the country have had it pretty tough economically. In fact, many of them have actually lost their farms; they've been repossessed by the banks.

"What makes it so difficult for those of us in this room is

that we know these people really well. Very few outsiders move into these communities, and very few people who were born and raised here ever move away. We've literally grown up with our customers. We went all the way through school with most of them. We go to church with them, we see them at the grocery store, and we work together in local service clubs. So you see, we'd feel pretty guilty if we were to go along with the owners' wishes and mark up the goods we sell 20% to 25%. After all, the people who own this business are rich. We see the kinds of cars they drive and the kinds of homes they live in. It's not fair, them making all that money and our friends and neighbors losing their farms right before our eyes."

After asking a few questions and listening to several opinions from the audience, I asked, "What retail store in this area do you feel offers the best value, you know, the most for your money?"

About five hands went up at once, and all five people said almost simultaneously, "Wal-Mart."

"How so?" I asked.

"Well, it's obvious. Their prices seem fair. They don't gouge their customers."

"I wonder what their mark-ups average," I asked.

"I don't know, but I'll bet they're a lot less than ours," my spokesperson shouted as if he were a Wal-Mart stockholder.

"I'll tell you what I'll do. When we break for lunch, I'll call the shareholder relations department at Wal-Mart's headquarters down in Arkansas and we'll find out. I'm sure their gross margin is public information," I told the group.

Everyone seemed pretty excited that this kind of information was available and even more so that we were going to be able to get an answer so soon.

When I called the Arkansas headquarters, I found out that Wal-Mart's gross margin was 22.8%, almost four percentage points higher than the retailer I was working for in the Midwest.

The audience was flabbergasted. They couldn't believe it. They realized for the first time that maybe the owners of their company weren't gouging their friends and neighbors with the prices they were charging.

In closing that day, I used a technique with the audience that I've used dozens of times. It went like this:

I turned the flip chart to a clean sheet of paper. At the top I wrote sales and put a plus sign to the left of sales. *(See Figure 4 on page 74.)*

From sales you subtract cost of goods sold and you will get gross profit.

From gross profit you subtract operating expenses. Of course, salaries and wages make up the majority of operating expenses, but other expenses include insurance, property taxes, office supplies, delivery expenses, and depreciation.

After you subtract operating expenses from gross profit, you are down to operating profit on the P&L.

To operating profit, you add other income. In most retail businesses, other income is made up of the service charges that are collected on past due accounts.

And from operating expenses you subtract other expenses. Other expenses are usually made up primarily of interest that the company must pay to lenders on borrowed funds.

This brings us down to pretax profit.

From pretax profit we subtract income taxes, and this calculation finally brings us down to the bottom line, or net profit, the amount the company takes to the bank.

Next, I ask the participants to tear from a writing pad a clean sheet of paper, and write down just one number. That number is the amount of money they believe that the cream of the crop, the best of the best, takes to the bank on a $100 sale.

After each participant has selected the amount of money these outstanding performers take to the bank, I ask them to fold the pieces of paper and pass them to the end of the table. I collect them, hand them to one of their coworkers, and ask him or her to call out the answers. As the numbers are called out, I write them on the board for all of the seminar participants to see.

Here are the typical responses I receive:

18; 22; 31; 19; 26; 10; 14; 21; 12; 9; 22; 15; 17; 11; 28

After going through this process, I reveal the correct answer. Industries vary, of course, but in the retail building supply industry, for example, the great majority of companies typically take only $2 to $4 to the bank on a $100 sale. And grocery stores, automobile dealers, and department stores (even Wal-Mart) often earn only around 1% to 3% after income taxes.

Guilt is the result of ignorance on the part of the individuals making pricing decisions. And who is responsible for this ignorance? I believe management should accept accountability. It's management's job to make sure all employees who either make pricing decisions or influence those decisions understand how critical it is to the company's bottom line to optimize gross margins. The above illustration is just one way to better educate employees.

An old friend and mentor of mine, South Florida business owner Lanny Moore, frequently uses the expression, "Business is business and romance is romance." What Lanny means is that friendship aside, managers and salespeople are paid to make money for the company. Yes, they are also hired to develop personal relationships with customers, but never to the detriment of profitability — the report card of the business world.

Webster's dictionary defines guilt as "a feeling of responsibility for having done something wrong." Employees must understand that there's nothing wrong with making a satisfactory profit. In fact, profitability is essential if a company expects to stay in business. So employees who feel guilty about charging a fair price for goods and services are contributing to the eventual demise of their company, and ultimately their own livelihood.

Figure 4. Exercise to illustrate how much net margin the most profitable companies take to the bank.

> + Sales
> — Cost of Goods Sold
> = Gross Profit
> — Operating Expenses
> = Operating Profit
> + Other Income
> — Other Expenses
> = Pretax Profit
> — Income Taxes
> = Net Profit or Net Margin
>   (The Bottom Line)

Factor #12
PRODUCT MIX

Virtually all companies, regardless of the industry, find they're able to earn higher gross margins on some product groups than on others. So it's essential that the sales force is motivated to sell the complete line rather than be allowed to concentrate on the product groups that are perhaps the most fun or the easiest to sell.

One technique is to have management sit down with the sales staff and agree on sales quotas not only for total sales, but also for specific product categories. I believe it's a mistake to give salespeople a free rein and allow them to sell whichever products they feel like selling and ignore the products in the line they don't wish to sell. After all, if the sales force won't sell the complete line, the company will fall short of its goals.

Here are the steps I recommend to my client base:

1. If I were the sales manager, I would first want each salesperson to do some research and tell me what dollar volume each existing customer and each prospect purchases by product line, regardless of the brand currently being purchased.

2. The next step is to ask each salesperson for an opinion on why each customer and prospect is not purchasing

certain products from our company.

3. The obstacles will vary. Once they are identified, I would design an action plan for each key customer and prospect.

4. Finally, I would ask each member of the sales force for a specific commitment expressed in dollars.

One of my clients was a New Jersey-based home center that had made a major commitment to Andersen Corp., a large national window manufacturer. A target account — builder Greg Boroski — was buying framing lumber from the company's outside sales rep but had never placed a window order. Instead, Boroski was buying a locally manufactured vinyl window.

1. *Potential sales volume.* The salesperson learned that Boroski bought approximately $500,000 in vinyl windows annually.

2. *Obstacle.* Boroski had been convinced that he could benefit more from the lower cost of the vinyl window than from the brand-name impact of a national manufacturer.

3. *Action plan.* Invite Boroski to visit the Andersen manufacturing facility in Bayport, Minn., go on a plant tour, and attend a seminar specially designed for builders. It was decided that it would be a good investment for the company's sales rep assigned to the account to accompany Boroski.

When Boroski and his sales rep arrived at the Minneapolis/St. Paul airport, they took a taxi to a hotel on the outskirts of town, where others who were in town for the plant tour and seminar were staying. That evening,

Andersen hosted a dinner for all the guests. Andersen and the sales rep had worked it out so that Boroski would sit next to a large builder with a fine national reputation who was a loyal Andersen customer. The two builders hit it off nicely. Boroski was told a lot about the benefits of installing a nationally known window brand by this Andersen customer. As an example, he learned how he could earn more gross margin on the homes he built and improve his company's image by using more national brands.

The next morning, after a big breakfast, the group was driven out to Bayport. Boroski had never been to Minnesota, so he enjoyed the drive. When they arrived at the Andersen manufacturing facility in Bayport, he was impressed with its size. The window and patio door manufacturing facility seemed to be as large as the entire town.

The group entered Andersen's headquarters, where several members of the Andersen executive staff — including the company president — mingled with the guests and welcomed them with coffee and sweet rolls.

Promptly at 9 a.m., the group moved into a seminar room, where Andersen's CEO and other executives formally welcomed them. The group learned that Andersen Corp. was the largest window manufacturer in the world; they heard how much money and time was dedicated to quality, research, and development. Boroski was again impressed.

Next on the agenda came a full-day seminar by Al Trellis of Maryland-based Home Builders Network. Trellis is well known for his expertise in the residential construction industry.

Afterward, the group was bused to the historic Lowell Inn in nearby Stillwater for dinner. Boroski met several more builders during the cocktail reception and dinner. He noticed everyone's willingness to discuss the details of their business, much of the conversation having nothing to do with windows. "Even if I never buy an Andersen brand window," he told one of the guests that evening, "this trip has certainly been worthwhile from a business perspective."

The next day, the group was bused to Bayport for a plant tour. They met craftsmen in the plant who were third- and fourth-generation Andersen employees. As the day went on, Boroski slowly became convinced that he had been missing a golden marketing opportunity. He began to realize that the climate in New Jersey especially lent itself to the benefits of vinyl-clad wood windows of the quality Andersen manufactured.

On the flight back to New Jersey, Boroski and his sales rep discussed how he could promote the Andersen brand to enhance the value Boroski's clients and prospects would perceive when they toured his models. The discussion evolved into a review of the pros and cons of incorporating more brand-name products into the homes he built.

While they were still on the plane, the sales rep got a firm commitment for his first Andersen order. The action plan worked. The sales rep was well on his way to improving his product mix with Boroski.

A client of mine in Florida has a sophisticated manufacturing operation to complement products he purchases for resale. While conducting a consulting assignment there a couple of years back, I performed an analysis to determine gross margin by category. The products the retailer manufactured on site generated substantially higher gross margins — 5 to 6 percent higher — than the commodity-type products purchased for stock.

I then analyzed the reports the company's computer system generated listing gross margin by salesperson. After ranking the sales staff by gross margin and cross-referencing to product categories, we found that some salespeople were selling an excellent product mix while others were selling primarily commodities.

The next step was to interview the salespeople at both extremes — those with both the highest and the lowest gross margins. The salespeople with the lowest gross margins confessed that they felt it was "too time-consuming" to sell the products the company manufactured and that there were too many problems associated with the higher-margin products.

The salespeople with the highest gross margins felt just the opposite. They had taken the time to pick up the product knowledge necessary to sell manufactured products. Their opinion was that there were few problems associated with these higher gross-margin products if you really understood the application and installation required and could communicate both effectively to the end user.

We arranged for the commodity-oriented salespeople to attend training classes conducted by a product specialist from the manufacturing division. In just a couple of months, these salespeople began to make great strides, and in four months, their product knowledge had soared. Next, they spent time in the field with customers observing how the manufactured products were installed. This enabled them to answer questions about installation more intelligently.

Since they already had a strong personal relationship with their existing customer base, it was relatively easy for the newly trained salespeople to expand their customer penetration. They convinced loyal customers to add manufactured products to the commodity products they were already buying.

Another tactic is to pay larger sales incentives — either in the form of commissions or spiffs — on the more-profitable product categories. *(See Chapter 25 on incentive compensation.)*

Anytime it's necessary to get salespeople's attention, monetary reward systems frequently work wonders. Most salespeople have relatively high economic values. As a group, they not only like money, they also like the material things money buys. This is one reason individuals with high economic values so frequently choose sales as a profession — they don't have to wait around for the boss to give them a raise. So if a company wishes to emphasize a particular product line, increasing the sales incentive on the products in that line is usually helpful.

In the case of the Florida client, commissions were increased from $2\frac{1}{2}\%$ to a full 4% for six months to get the sales force's attention. Meticulous records were maintained, and the extra commission was paid in a separate check so the salespeople could readily see the financial benefits of their success.

Additional sales training is probably the most effective way to help salespeople sell a more diverse product mix. The more profitable product lines are often more technical in nature, and therefore more time-consuming and complicated to sell. Salespeople who have yet to master the product knowledge or the selling skills to convince customers to buy the total package frequently take a path-of-least-resistance approach to selling and concentrate only on products that have commodity characteristics.

Factor #13
CUSTOMER MIX

All companies have some customers who are more profitable to do business with than others. Most business owners and managers agree that it's not wise to completely avoid customers who come under the heading of "low-margin accounts." But unless your company has been successful at becoming the market's low-cost producer, it's also wise to sprinkle in a significant number of customers who don't use lowball pricing as their sole criterion in selecting a supplier.

The consultant, author, and seminar leader Larry Steinmetz has some good advice on this: "Avoid price buyers. Unless you've geared your business toward servicing companies and consumers who buy strictly on price, you're better off staying away from them. They will eat you alive by demanding every last ounce of service you have to give, but are never willing to pay for [those services]."

Many stories have been published about manufacturers that have gone broke allowing retailers like Wal-Mart or The Home Depot to capture too much of their manufacturing capacity. The sales potential is appealing, but let's face it: Most category-killers are price buyers. They have to be, because so much of their marketing plan centers around price. Because they have so little service to offer, they have to survive on either real or perceived lowball pricing.

Because some customers are just naturally more profitable than others — to optimize gross margins — salespeople must adopt a marketing plan that calls for selling a more diverse customer base. I'm not advocating that manufacturers, distributors, and retailers avoid selling "price buyers" altogether, but I am suggesting that a company's marketing plan should include a respectable mix of customers and prospects who value quality and service.

As a rule of thumb, larger and highly aggressive customers have enough clout to demand lower prices, which yield lower gross margins. But by the same token, smaller, less aggressive customers will usually yield much higher gross margins. So a marketing plan that is successful at attracting a good mix of large, medium, and small customers will usually produce a satisfactory level of sales, at a more attractive gross margin than a plan that is too narrowly focused around price buyers.

While it's important to take into consideration the economies of scale that the larger-volume customers make possible, this group of customers frequently requires fewer services than smaller customers. So to attract a more profitable customer base, you may find it effective to use services as a marketing tool; that is, provide services for your smaller customers that they can't afford to provide for themselves.

EXAMPLES

1. Many wholesale distributors offer pricing services whereby a price label accompanies each inventory item the wholesaler ships to the retailer.

2. It's not at all unusual for manufacturers, wholesalers, and retailers to offer educational seminars to their customer base.

3. Conduct product knowledge training programs.

4. Have your organization's marketing or sales manager help customers put together their marketing plans.

5. If applicable, encourage your customers to invite their customers to tour your facilities.

6. Offer your sales staff's services to your customers. For example, offer to allow them to take an inventory of the products they sell the customer. It helps the customer avoid out-of-stocks, and it puts the salesperson in a position to know at all times the exact status of the products he sells that customer.

7. If you have customers who are experiencing financial challenges, offer to have your company's CFO take a look at their financial statements and make suggestions.

Larger customers and prospects may have departments and staff to perform many of the services they need. Smaller customers, on the other hand, may be dependent on their suppliers or other providers for the kinds of services they cannot justify providing internally. Therefore, your marketing plan must address several sizes and classes of customers.

Educational seminars, technical services, financing, small-quantity deliveries, client referrals, special-order material, product specialists, and consignment inventories are services that smaller customers frequently need. Larger customers may want some of these services, but they don't necessarily need them. Of course, each of these services bears a cost that must be considered when you calculate your costs of doing business.

CUSTOMER CATEGORIZATION

In order to manage gross margin more effectively, many successful companies categorize their customer and prospect base both by size and by function. In other words, large customers who perform many of the essential business functions internally might receive a particular designation. Medium-size customers who perform only a few of the service-related functions in-house would receive another designation. And smaller customers who are almost totally dependent on suppliers or who farm out all but basic functions would receive yet another designation. The names for these designations vary from company to company, but it is important to look at customer categorization from a pricing perspective.

THE ROBINSON-PATMAN ACT

Another reason manufacturers set up classes of trade was the Robinson-Patman Act, which became law in 1936. The law has been enforced by some administrations and almost completely ignored by others. But no book on gross margin control would be complete without at least a perfunctory mention of the Robinson-Patman Act and how it has influenced pricing in the United States.

Large national chains and the national buying groups often pay lower prices than single-location stores because of competitive factors. But by virtue of the Robinson-Patman Act, manufacturers are not allowed to lateralize pricing from one customer to another; that is, they may not arbitrarily extend the price one customer is receiving to one of the customer's competitors, unless the lower price is extended to all competitors in the same trade area. Because so many suppliers attempt to follow this law, each customer must shop the market, talk to the various manufacturers, and communicate to its preferred supplier if a competitor is quoting a lower price than the preferred supplier is charging. The law allows suppliers to meet a specific competitive situation with a particular customer without extending the same price to other customers in a given trade area.

In my opinion, the Robinson-Patman Act is almost impossible to avoid violating. Not only is it inflationary, it costs manufacturers a fortune to maintain the paperwork to document that they are not lateralizing pricing when they decide to lower a price for a customer.

However, by the same token, Robinson-Patman provides a magnificent cop-out for manufacturers. Whenever a retailer complains that a competitor is selling the manufacturer's product at ridiculously low prices and accuses the manufacturer of not keeping them competitive, the vendor can always use the law as an excuse: "Sorry, we're not allowed to divulge our pricing to our other customers. If, however, you are successful in getting one of our bona fide competitors to quote you a lower price, we'll be happy to take it under advisement."

Another provision is this: If a manufacturer does lower a price to a customer without documentation that it is meeting a specific competitive situation, then that manufacturer is required to extend that same lower price to each company with whom that customer is competing for business. This provision makes it necessary for all manufacturers and suppliers to set up specific trade areas that they can defend in the geographical regions they serve. In 1936, the U.S. population was much more sparse, so trade areas didn't overlap as much as they do today. The larger and more dense the population, the more difficult it is to establish trade areas that don't overlap.

The original purpose of the Robinson-Patman Act ostensibly was to protect smaller companies from being run out of business by far larger competitors with much greater buying power. More specifically, it was enacted so that businesses on the same functional level would stand on an equal competitive footing with respect to price. But because of the provision in the law that a supplier is allowed to "meet specific competitive quotations" with one customer without being required to extend that same price to all customers in the trade area, the law is not only time-consuming and expensive to obey — it's ineffective, as well.

As an example, I'll explain how my old industry, the asphalt roofing products industry, segmented its customers. Manufacturers frequently set up all customers under these kinds of designations. As I recall, we sold the following classes of trade:

1. National retail chains.

2. National buying groups.

3. Regional buying groups.

4. Stocking distributors.

5. Independent retailers.

6. Independent roofing contractors.

National chains and national buying groups almost always ended up qualifying for the lowest price. This was true partly because they had such tremendous buying power. Another factor was that they were large enough to buy from just about all manufacturers. They had so many locations that they had the luxury of spreading their business around. With so many manufacturers trying to increase their market share in these large national accounts, the national chains and the national buying groups had little difficulty documenting lower prices. This gave manufacturers the documentation for their files to satisfy Robinson-Patman.

Another reason manufacturers could frequently justify lower prices to national accounts was because they required less selling effort in the field. A national account manager was usually assigned to service the home office, and the field sales force was used strictly for servicing product complaints, supplying samples, and conducting training sessions.

If, however, a manufacturer was selling large national account customers exclusively, its bottom line would almost certainly suffer. So to take a rifle shot at the other categories, they had to have a field sales force dedicated to servicing the other classes of trade — regional buying groups, stocking distributors, independent retailers, and independent roofing contractors.

Stocking distributors usually received a "functional" discount that theoretically compensated them for the stocking and reselling "function." Stocking distributors or wholesalers would stock the manufacturer's merchandise, field their own sales force, and redistribute the material to smaller retailers and roofers who could not justify buying in carload or truckload quantities shipped directly from the factory.

Functional discounts vary by industry and by manufacturer, but our net selling price to stocking distributors almost always generated a higher gross margin than we could earn by selling national accounts.

The highest gross margins were generated by selling relatively small independent retailers and independent roofers, those either unaffiliated with a buying group or who chose not to purchase through a buying group. Even though most of these independents belonged to national or regional buying groups, many of them were so "independent" that their buyers resisted giving up advantages they perceived by maintaining a direct relationship with the manufacturer. Sometimes it was the buyers' egos that got in the way, but other times it was because the buyers sincerely

believed they were more skilled buyers than their counter-
parts in the buying groups.

Of course the buying groups must take some of the
blame for their members' choosing to bypass them and deal
directly with the manufacturer. Most buying groups invoice
their members at what the buying group and the manufacturer jointly agree to be "market price." Then the buying
group issues a rebate to the member (independent retailer
or roofer) either quarterly or annually. The specific amount
of the rebate, however, is often so highly confidential that
the buyer is not privileged to know what it is. So when a
manufacturer quotes a buyer a lower price than what
appears on the buying group's invoice, the buyer often figures that "a bird in the hand" is better than a secret rebate.

In addition to complying with Robinson-Patman, however, manufacturers also play pricing games to muddy the
waters enough to eke out higher gross margins.

Most suppliers segment their customer bases. Office
supply companies, for example, certainly sell relatively
large corporations at lower prices than they sell smaller
businesses that buy only a fraction of the large companies'
volume. To generate larger gross margins from smaller
businesses, many office suppliers will sell a small business
on purchasing a full year's supply of, say, letterhead. A
year's supply is often a great enough quantity to lower costs
sufficiently to allow the supplier to sell at a highly competitive price with a negligible effect on gross margin. The
small business is then allowed to pull letterhead from stock
— and pay for it — when its in-house supply needs to be
replenished.

Computer supply retailers often negotiate contracts
with larger customers that are tied to sales volume. And
copier sales and service companies frequently tie their pricing structure to the number of machines they have under
maintenance agreements.

Full-line building supply businesses (as opposed to specialty houses that sell only limited classes of trade) often segment their customer bases as follows:

1. Large production building contractors.
2. Large custom building contractors.
3. Smaller custom building contractors.
4. Repair and remodeling contractors.
5. Commercial and industrial accounts.
6. Consumers.

The lowest gross margins usually are generated by large production or tract building contractors who purchase $1 million or more in annual volume. The highest gross margins come from Mr. or Mrs. Jones, who walk into the store looking for one board or one piece of plywood. As a rule of thumb, sales to professional buyers with a lot of buying power generally yield a lower gross margin than sales to amateurs who need a lot of expensive sales assistance in determining the right product for a given project. Of course, costs go up when the volume a sale generates is low and the level of service required to make the sale is high.

SPECIALIZATION

In densely populated metropolitan areas, more and more retailers are finding that they must specialize. The luxury of specialization allows a retailer to focus on a particular class of trade and outservice competitors that are attempting to be all things to all people. So the decision to specialize not only can become a marketing advantage, but also gives retailers an opportunity to gear their business toward the specific needs of a particular class of trade. When a market is large enough to make specialization practical, higher gross margins are usually generated.

SALES QUOTAS

When a retailer uses a field sales force to move goods to market, sales quotas tied to each class of trade serviced is an effective way to make sure sales reps focus on customers and prospects at all levels. If the sales reps meet their quota, odds are that the company will achieve an optimal gross margin.

SALES SPECIALISTS

If a retailer's customer classes are too unusual or specialized for the same sales rep to service all of them, converting to sales specialists is often a viable option. This is especially true in industries where a high degree of technical expertise is necessary to service key customer groups.

The key to customer mix as a factor to optimize gross margins is to make sure your company and its sales personnel are selling a good mix of customers, not merely selling the customers that are the easiest to sell. Otherwise, gross margins will suffer and the retailer will have to pay more attention to expense control, cost-cutting, and perhaps even downsizing.

Factor #14
AVOID OUT-OF-STOCKS

Buyers are usually accountable for inventory control; that is, optimizing inventory turnover. But buyers also must be held accountable for holding another inventory measurement to a minimum — out-of-stocks. When buyers manage inventory so tightly that they run out of stock, it's like a running back stepping on the out-of-bounds line during a long kickoff return.

Being out of stock has a negative impact on gross margin and customer service.

1. Out-of-stocks almost always inconvenience the customer.

2. In companies with a strong commitment to customer service, a more expensive product may have to be substituted but sold at the same price as the one that's out of stock.

3. If no substitute product is available from inventory, in order to serve the customer, a retailer may have to buy the product from a competitor, possibly creating a sale at break-even or zero gross profit.

4. Inability to make the product available on a timely basis may cause the company to inconvenience its customer.

5. When out-of-stocks occur too frequently, customers lose confidence in a merchant's ability to service the account.

Surveys show that one of the primary benefits the public perceives in doing business with large category-killers is their reputation for keeping most items in stock. When consumers feel confident that a retailer will have a good supply of what they're looking for, their tendency is to go out of their way to do business there.

Here is an example. After a routine visit to my family doctor, I was sent to a local lab for blood tests. One was a routine PSA test which can detect the possibility of prostate cancer. My PSA came back slightly elevated, so my doctor sent me to a urologist for several punch biopsies. When the biopsy results came back, I got the shock of my life — I had prostate cancer. After much research and angst, my wife and I reached the conclusion that I should have my prostate gland removed. The surgery went well, and after three days in the hospital I was able to go home.

One of the side effects of prostate surgery is incontinence. So I had to wear adult Depends™ for a few weeks. My wife bought the first supply at Phar-Mor, a large discount drugstore, but when I needed to replenish my supply, I went to Revco, a drugstore that's part of a national chain. There was a space on the shelf marked "Adult Depends," but it was empty. The store was out of stock. A bit irked that I was inconvenienced, I tried Eckerd, another chain-operated drugstore. Same story; the manager said they normally carried them, but they were out of stock. So I drove back across town to Phar-Mor, where they had a full supply on the shelf.

Because I imagine that Depends is a relatively high gross-margin product for drugstores and grocers, both stores that I tried to do business with lost out on a gross margin-enhancing opportunity by being out of stock.

Because my recovery required that I not work for almost two months, a week or so later, my wife and I decided to spend a couple of weeks at Kiawah Island, a South Carolina resort near Charleston. When I needed another supply of Depends, I drove to Rite Aid, the local chain-operated drugstore and the one closest to where we were staying. Would you believe it? The label on the shelf indicated that the store carried them, but the shelf was empty. So I was forced to drive 10 miles to a Wal-Mart that had a full supply in stock.

Here's another example. One of my "honey-dos" during my recovery was to replace the old showerhead in our bathroom. I had already bought the showerhead, but when I got ready to install it, I realized that I didn't have a wrench large enough to do the job. Since my dad owned a hardware store for so many years, I look for almost any opportunity to go into an old-fashioned hardware store. I drove past a local chain store on Johns Island, Builders FirstSource, to visit a recently renovated local hardware store. But they were out of stock on the adjustable wrench I was looking for. How can a hardware store stay in business when it is out of stock on a basic item like an adjustable wrench, I wondered. I drove back to Builders FirstSource and found precisely the wrench I was looking for.

Just like most consumers, I am a busy person, so — as much as I enjoy the atmosphere of a hardware store — I was unimpressed enough with that store's total disregard for its inventory of hand tools that I won't waste my time going there again. In the future, I'll do business at Builders FirstSource.

Most retailers have more money tied up in inventory than any other asset, so it's certainly wise to manage it carefully. But when a store develops a reputation among its customer base of not being a reliable source of supply, most customers won't continue to shop there. Gross margin suffers, and so do sales. The point is this: Most people are too busy these days to waste time shopping a store that doesn't have an efficient enough inventory control system to stay in stock. When a customer is inconvenienced two or three times, he or she will mark that particular store off their list.

BUYER INCENTIVES

Most buyers receive a bonus based on their ability to achieve optimal inventory turns, but few have any sort of incentive plan based on out-of-stocks. I believe this is a mistake.

Home Depot has a reputation for lousy customer service, but it also has an excellent reputation for usually being in-stock on the tens of thousands of items carried. The chain pays its departmental personnel a special incentive when they are not out-of-stock on any items in their department for an entire quarter. The incentive is not a huge amount of money, but it does send a clear message that out-of-stocks are not good for business.

Making sure your store holds out-of-stocks to a minimum is every employee's job. Anytime an employee notices that a shelf or bin is below a measurably acceptable level, a responsible manager or buyer should be alerted. It's impossible for a company to predict when so much of a given item will be bought that the stock is depleted. After all, that's what a retail store is for, to service its customers. But just because a store runs out is no excuse for staying out.

I recommend that my clients set out-of-stock goals for both buyers and customer service personnel and reward those people when they succeed at avoiding out-of-stocks.

There are several ways to minimize the negative impact of being out-of-stock. Many retailers advertise that they will reorder any item and call the customer when it comes in. If the customer doesn't need the item immediately, this is an excellent customer service idea.

A great example of this kind of service is Fowler's

Pharmacy, a family-owned and managed drugstore just a few blocks from my home in Greenville, S.C. I don't know how they do it, but Fowler's Pharmacy has incredibly quick access to just about anything you could ever need from a drugstore. If it's out of stock on an item you're looking for, it has a special arrangement with a wholesaler that provides delivery within 24 hours. Sometimes it's even the same day. The best part of the service is that when the item you ordered comes in, it will be delivered to your home at no additional charge.

When a retailer provides this kind of service, I'm happy to pay more. I believe most people would agree.

Try this: Don't attempt to be all things to all people. If you decide to buy a new line of products, buy enough stock for your customers to know that you've really made a commitment. When a customer sees only one or two products on each pegboard hook or shelf, it looks as if the retailer either can't afford a deep inventory or hasn't really made a commitment. I would rather see fewer categories of merchandise with a full commitment than many categories that look too skimpy.

Your customers need to feel fairly certain that you'll have what they're looking for or, regardless of how good your customer service is, they'll stop coming back.

Factor #15
VARIABLE PRICING

As a consumer, I don't like it when retailers I do business with adopt a variable pricing strategy, that is, use "loss leaders" to lure me into their store. When I fall prey to such a pricing strategy, I feel tricked. I hate that feeling of being misled.

On the rare occasion that I visit a Sam's Club store, it's usually because my wife has invited me to come along to help carry several cases of dog food out to the car. On one of these occasions, I spotted a case of my favorite brand of beer — Miller Lite — sitting on a shelf as we entered the store. The price tag was printed in large letters: $9.85.

Wow! I said to myself, this place is terrific. I'm accustomed to paying about $13.50 at the local supermarket. So I bought two cases. (My reward to myself each day for exercising is two 12-ounce cans of Miller Lite beer, so I figured that I'd load up with a 24-day supply.)

When my supply of beer ran low, I asked my wife to accompany me back to Sam's Club, since she has the only membership card in our family. I could hardly wait to rack up some more great savings. But when I walked into the store this time, I noticed that there was no Miller Lite sitting on the shelf in the front of the store.

"Oh, well," I thought as I walked towards the back of the store, "I'm sure they still have a great deal."

When I arrived at the beer and wine area, I couldn't believe my eyes: There was a big sign hanging over the Miller Lite that read: Case $13.30.

Although I was disappointed, I thought, "You dummy. In your seminars you teach variable pricing, and now you've been a victim of it." I'm living proof that variable pricing does work. It worked on me. It especially works for retailers who cater to consumers.

It can work for non-consumer-oriented retailers, as well. In many markets, it's not uncommon for business-to-business retailers to sell some commodities practically at cost in order to get a customer's attention, then turn around and make up the difference on less price-sensitive items.

After all, it's the overall gross margin that the total sale produces that's important, not necessarily what you earn on each individual item the customer buys.

THE RAZOR AND THE BLADES

Another pricing technique that takes advantage of this concept is frequently referred to as the "razor and the blades." Gillette may practically give away the razor in order to induce consumers to buy one, but what good is a razor without blades? If you could see Gillette's gross margin by product, I'll bet that its overall gross margin is quite satisfactory when the gross margin on razors and blades is averaged.

ISLANDS OF LOSSES AMID SEAS OF PROFITS

When we research some of the nation's most successful retailers, we frequently find that price-driven retailers who use variable pricing techniques actually have higher overall gross margins than retailers that are more service-oriented and use more traditional pricing techniques. The reason is that for every product they offer at a lowball price, they offer dozens of others that produce top dollar. If you shop stores that use this pricing tactic, you'll usually find "islands of losses amid seas of profits."

One of my clients in Oregon heard that a California-based discount store had bought land and was planning to enter his market. The closest store he could find was in California, so he and his team bit the bullet and drove down to pay a visit to the soon-to-be competitor. With the help of a supplier, they shopped all the products in the store.

"What shocked us," the client said, "was not how many prices were lower than ours, but rather how many of our prices we were actually able to increase." When the discount store did arrive, the locally owned retailer was ready. He put together a well-thought-out and well-designed variable pricing plan that was highly effective. After just a couple of years, the competitor closed its doors and pulled out of the market.

As I said earlier, I personally don't like stores that employ variable pricing techniques. But variable pricing is a lot like the negative political ads on television. Everyone complains about how dirty politics is, but poll after poll indicates that the public is influenced by negative ads. They work. And so does variable pricing.

If your business sells consumers, it's almost imperative these days to establish some sort of variable pricing scheme. Variable pricing is all about image — the image your customers have of the prices your business charges for the merchandise it sells. When price-conscious customers see an item that they're familiar with priced at what they perceive to be a super bargain, it has a psychological impact. Call it naive, call it gullible, but they tend to believe that the business has some sort of secret that enables them to sell cheaper than the competition.

Although variable pricing can be effective in just about

any business, it works best when the business caters to consumers and when the business sells merchandise that its
customers don't purchase every day. Most consumers, for
example, purchase a new storm door for their home only
every few years. Therefore, off the top of his head, the average homeowner wouldn't know the price a store typically
charges for a storm door.

Grocery stores, on the other hand, don't have the same
luxury. Most people who routinely shop for groceries have
at least a ballpark idea of the cost of a box of laundry deter-
gent, a pound of ground beef, a jar of applesauce, or a package of Oreos. So you'll notice that while grocery stores do
advertise the price of individual items, you're probably not
as blown away by their specials as you might be at a store
you visit less often.

Another technique that some retailers find effective is to
variably price products their customers purchase on a frequent basis, but not products that their store is known for.
This is why you'll often see gas stations with a mountain-
high stack of six-packs of Coke priced at below cost sitting
out front. Of course, you usually are allowed to buy only
one six-pack at the sale price for every eight gallons of gas
you buy. In summer, home centers might advertise a truckload sale of charcoal and lighter fluid that they sell at below
cost to build traffic. Restaurants often sell T-shirts imprinted with their logo at cost or below cost. Motor oil is another favorite loss leader for many retailers. The theory is:
Screw up somebody else's market. Use another merchant's
products as a loss leader, not your own.

Since illusion plays such a big part in the effectiveness
of a variable pricing plan, it helps to associate an item you
have priced at cost or below cost with a believable event
that the public will buy into. The following are some examples:

1. We're passing along to our customers some of the savings because we bought a boatload, a truckload, or a railcar load.

2. We bought too much and have to dump the excess to raise cash. Our loss is your gain.

3. Our buyers just returned from a buying trip to Indonesia.

4. We just returned from a buying show where we picked up some incredible deals.

5. We're closing out last year's models to make room for next year's models.

Big, bold displays add to the effectiveness of a variable pricing plan. Make your displays of loss leaders impressive, with product stacked out in front of your store and spilling out into the parking lot. Make the display look as if you cornered the world market on whatever it is you're selling at such an unusually low price.

Of course, no company ever enhanced gross margin from variable pricing schemes alone. The only purpose of variable pricing is to build traffic. Once you have the people in your store, they must buy other items with above-average gross margins or your company will lose its shirt. *(See Chapter 8 on add-on selling and Chapter 16 on merchandising.)*

Factor #16
EFFECTIVE (AND CLEVER) ADVERTISING AND MERCHANDISING

I'll begin with some of the most effective merchandising techniques I've observed. When I stand in the checkout line at a supermarket or at just about any retail store, for that matter, I rarely see low-margin commodity-type products on display. If you'll observe closely the next time you're in line, you'll see similar sorts of high-margin impulse items. You know what I'm talking about — those items that you didn't intend to buy, but that have a certain amount of customer appeal. The following are several examples that I ran across in one grocery store:

1. Candy
2. Magazines
3. Tabloids
4. Batteries
5. Chewing gum
6. Disposable razors
7. Key rings
8. Miniature flashlights
9. Nail clippers

In your store, identify the impulse items you have in stock and make sure they are near the checkout lanes. Your gross margin will improve as a result.

While it's a good idea to use loss leaders to increase store traffic, it's equally effective to attractively display your higher-margin premium products so that customers will have difficulty deciding between lower-margin bargains and brand-name products that are better-looking, more prestigious, longer-lasting, higher-quality — and carry higher gross margins.

While it's wise to intermingle bargain products on end cap displays, end caps should also call attention to your highest-quality and best-margin items.

Change end cap displays often. It's a mistake for your store to be so predictable that your regular customers begin to take your store for granted. Displays should change often enough for the store to have a fresh look to even your most dependable customers.

"AS ADVERTISED" SIGNS

Make good use of "as advertised" signs around your store. You don't necessarily have to beat the competition's prices, but whenever someone in your market runs an ad on an item you're willing to sell for their advertised price, put an "as advertised" sign on it. When customers see the "as advertised" sign, they realize that it must be a good buy, if not a bargain.

Good merchandising is somewhat of an art. By "art," I mean not every employee on your payroll is going to be effective at putting together attractive displays. The best store merchandisers have a flare for decorating. They can visualize what type of display will fit both the space allotted and the product itself.

I'm not an especially gifted merchandiser. As an example, I'm weak when it comes to what colors go best together. If I want to dress up for a special occasion, I would never go to a men's store to select a new outfit. I know my limitations. On the other hand, my wife, Patti, is extremely gifted at all kinds of decorating, whether it's me or the family room that needs a makeover. So I leave the aesthetic aspects of our relationship to her.

In years past — before Patti and I met — I discovered a way to be well-dressed in spite of my inability to put an outfit together. You may think of this technique as cheating, but it worked for me. I would visit some of the finest men's clothing stores and study the clothes they used to dress the mannequins in the front window, assuming, of course, that the store had a sharp merchandiser on staff.

This same technique works in a retail store. If you or your store personnel lack the innate skills to attractively merchandise your store, it's a great idea to visit extremely well-merchandised retail stores that sell merchandise similar to yours.

Anytime I travel in the United States, Canada, or Europe, I make it a routine part of my trip to visit as many shops and outlets as I can. My wife's fondness for shopping makes this part of our trip something we can both enjoy. To better remember the good merchandising ideas I observe, I carry a handheld dictation device that holds a 30-minute mini cassette. There are several brands of dictation devices on the market, but the Lanier brand is my personal favorite. The Lanier unit is among the most expensive on the market, but I believe it's also the best, most dependable, and the easiest to use.

If you feel conspicuous standing in the middle of a retail store speaking into a recorder, the Lanier unit is so small that it will easily fit into a shirt or jacket pocket. And the microphone is so sensitive that you can turn on the recorder, leave it in your pocket, and it will pick up your comments even if you speak in a normal voice. To keep from wasting audiotape, I frequently hold my hand on the Lanier unit in my jacket pocket, turning it on and off as I move from area to area in the store.

I do my best to describe every detail of the product display so I'll have enough detailed information to reconstruct the display when I get home.

If you're committed to improving your merchandising skills, make this practice a habit. When you get back to your office, have your dictations typed so you can edit them while your observations are still fresh in your mind. I've found it convenient to file these merchandising write-ups by product category. In a few years you'll be surprised at how extensive your merchandising files will be.

Earlier I mentioned traveling in Europe. While the United States and Canada seem to have done a pretty good job of stealing each other's ideas, European retailers have come up with some unique innovations. I found that the same was true on a trip I made several years ago to Australia.

I believe exposure is perhaps the best education any business person will ever receive — exposure to different ways of merchandising in other cities, states, provinces, and countries. In a particular company, no matter how innovative the people in the organization are, you have a finite amount of merchandising talent. But when your personnel are exposed to innovative ideas that other retailers have found to be effective, their own creativity often goes into overdrive.

Several years ago, my firm was hired by Jerry's, a Eugene, Ore.-based retailer, to recruit a merchandising manager. I was impressed when the owner, Dennis Orem, told me that in that particular year his company budgeted more than $50,000 for him and his key merchandising personnel to travel all over North America looking for new merchandising techniques. "We are well aware that Eugene is not a merchandising mecca, so to stay ahead of the competition we have to get out and learn what other successful retailers are doing," Orem told me.

Another of my clients, Buena Park Lumber & Hardware (now Ganahl Lumber) in Orange County, Calif., has taken a lesson from Cracker Barrel and other merchants who have been able to differentiate their retail establishment from competitors. Buena Park has built dozens of attractive display areas within the store. It's difficult not to buy something as you walk through the store and take in its uniqueness.

Another example of this merchandising technique is The Fresh Market, a Greensboro, N.C.-based grocery store chain. When you walk into the store you notice that it's smaller than a traditional grocery store. The fragrance makes you realize that the store is different. Old-fashioned-looking sacks of flour, rice, and potatoes are stacked on a mezzanine. Sitting on the floor are open crates that contain bulk quantities of vegetables. Fresh herb plants are always available in the spring and summer. None of the meat products are pre-packaged. Rather, butchers are available to serve customers at a meat counter.

One of my favorite advertising and promotion consultants is Columbus, Ohio-based Jeff Slutsky. Slutsky is the author of *Streetfighting: Low-Cost Advertising/Promotions For Your Business.* (To order, call 800-758-8759, or visit *www.streetfighter.com.*)

The product specials advertised by the so-called "category killers" can be a real detriment to the gross margins more service-oriented retailers are able to achieve. In his seminars, Slutsky tells a story about the time he was hired by an independently owned major appliance retailer. Slutsky's mission was to help the store reduce the number of consumers who "shopped" the independent retailer to take advantage of the knowledgeable staff, but then drove down the street to buy the appliance from a discounter at a lower price.

Slutsky suggested that the store fill one of its freezers with several flavors of ice cream. The floor sales staff was instructed to be as polite and courteous to customers as possible. They were told to answer all of the prospects' questions to the best of their ability. But before a seriously interested prospect left the store, the salesperson would offer him or her a half gallon of ice cream as a small thank you for coming by.

Especially on hot summer days, Slutsky's suggestion worked like a charm. A significant percentage of visitors to the appliance store went straight home, not wanting their ice cream to melt. At this appliance store, this counter-tactic resulted in fewer prospects driving down the street to compare the appliance retailer's prices against those at the discount store.

Another of Slutsky's advertising innovations concerned a local pizza shop that used a relatively small ad in the Yellow Pages to attract business. When a large pizza chain came to town, however, the new competitor purchased a full page Yellow Page ad on the page immediately across from the local pizza merchant's small ad.

Slutsky came up with a brilliant idea. He suggested that the local pizza shop run a special radio ad that made the following offer: "Bring in a copy of the pizza chain's full page ad and get a special deal — buy one pizza and get a second pizza FREE."

After a few weeks, a big percentage of the local telephone books no longer contained the chain's full-page ad.

Factor #17
EXCLUSIVE PRODUCT OFFERINGS

Seek out exclusive product offerings to avoid a competitive rat race. Any time a retailer can offer a product that's not available from competitors in the marketplace, there's an opportunity to optimize gross margin.

Neiman Marcus, the well-known Texas-based retailer, is famous for this technique. Their buyers spend many days each year traveling in Third World countries looking for unique products they can purchase on an exclusive basis.

Other retailers will resort to "private labeling" to avoid being forced to compete with the same brands discount retailers use as loss leaders. Many times, nationally known paint manufacturers such as Glidden and Sherwin-Williams will also make their products available under a retailer's own private brand. Same paint, but different label.

Sears is one of the world's pioneers in private labeling. Kenmore appliances and Craftsman tools are examples of Sears' private brands that have become so well-known that the public now has as much confidence in Sears' private brands as they had in national non-exclusive brands.

Some of the nation's larger hardware and building material buying cooperatives such as Ace Hardware, Do It Best Corp., and TruServ offer their member stores this opportunity to build brand-name recognition — and increase gross margins. Some, such as Ace, have even acquired their own paint manufacturing plants.

The Home Depot has taken this strategy a step further by convincing some national manufacturers to make products to the giant home center's own specifications. While, for example, a particular brand of a $1/_4$-inch power drill may appear to be identical to a $1/_4$-inch drill an unsuspecting consumer might have priced in another retail store, closer inspection will reveal that this may not be the case. The consumer may find that the Home Depot drill is manufactured somewhat differently; say, with a shorter cord.

In 1997, Lowe's Companies, the North Wilkesboro, N.C.-based home center chain, pulled off a real coup to set it apart from its competitors. It negotiated an exclusive arrangement with Olympic — nationally known for its line of stains — to manufacture Olympic-brand paint products.

Because the 700-plus store retailer was the only retailer in the nation to offer PPG Industries' Olympic-brand paints, it was insulated against price-comparison competition between national brands, thus preventing gross margin erosion. In 2002, Lowe's operated in 42 states.

While retailers in the past have had territorially exclusive deals with vendors for certain product lines, the Lowe's-PPG agreement takes retailer exclusivity to a new level. Lowe's new captive label differs from many retailers in that they are taking a brand name already familiar to their customers and attaching to it a new product category.

While exclusivity is a powerful factor that enhances gross margin, it's usually short-lived. Eventually, competitors will figure out a way to get their hands on the brand.

Factor #18
SCRUTINIZE GROSS MARGIN REPORTS

Computer systems can be incredibly strong gross-margin-management tools when managers diligently scrutinize the sales and gross margin reports their system generates.

When retail owners and managers first computerized their businesses back in the late '70s and early '80s, they treated the system's sales and gross margin reports like a kid with a new toy. It was not unusual to hear of managers sitting up until all hours of the night poring over reports that gave them information they would have had to spend countless hours accumulating before computerizing. But as time passed, there was a tendency to take those reports for granted and allow them to pile up in a corner of the office — a costly decision.

Computer systems these days generate sales and gross profit reports by a dozen or more different categories, such as:

- Outside salesperson
- Inside salesperson
- Department
- Major product category
- Minor product category
- Individual product or sku

- ❒ Individual customer
- ❒ Customer class
- ❒ Job or project
- ❒ By promotional event

One of the biggest mistakes I see retailers making is allowing their financial personnel to select the company's computer system. More often than not, financial and administrative staff have an entirely different agenda than do sales, marketing, and line management.

I remember one client many years ago that handed over the computer software selection process to its chief financial officer. I was VP of marketing and sales at Enterprise Computer Systems Inc. and accompanied our salesperson on the sales call. When the salesperson — representing our industry-specific system — began demonstrating the features of the system, he decided to begin with inventory control and gross margin control, the system modules that would allow the retailer to generate the highest return on his investment very quickly.

This turned out to be a mistake that ultimately cost us the sale. About a quarter of the way into the demo, the CFO stopped the salesperson and said, "All of those inventory and gross margin reports are nice-to-haves, but our main concern is not ever again having to manually prepare a journal entry."

With few exceptions, I've found that just about any company's computer system can run payroll, accounts payable, and general ledger. But those system modules rarely put enough additional profit on the bottom line to justify the cost of the system. It is enhanced gross margin control and inventory control that give the retailer the timely information needed to make a big difference in profitability.

My favorite gross margin reports:

Daily sales register. The daily sales register lists each transaction that was processed through the point of sales system. It doesn't take long to peruse the daily sales register. We teach our clients to slowly run their index finger down the gross margin column on this report. Keep an eye out for any gross margins that look unusually high or unusually low. If you can't justify a gross margin that appears on the daily sales report, it pays to go to the original invoice for additional information. If a pricing mistake was made on a charge sale, it is advisable to "back out" the invoice and reinvoice at the correct price.

Gross margin exception report. When each sku is set up in the system, the software asks for the minimum gross margin that's acceptable on that particular inventory item. Then when the gross margin exception report is run at the end of the day, it alerts the manager to any line item on an invoice that was sold at an unacceptable gross margin. We recommend that an employee be designated to research every item that appears on the gross margin exception report.

Caution: Be realistic when you set the minimum margins. If too many line items appear on the gross margin exception report, managers will be so overwhelmed that they won't take the necessary time to scrutinize this report. If a particular item is highly competitive and has to be sold at rock-bottom prices that yield, say, only a 6% gross margin, make sure the software is set at 2% or 3% so that it won't be an exception every time that product is sold.

Special-order sales. On special-order items, we recommend that the meter be set at 99% so that every special-order sale prints on this report. Special-order pricing is so often abused that we believe sales personnel should know that they are going to be asked to justify any special-order sale that doesn't yield a satisfactory gross margin.

Gross margin by salesperson. This report clearly identifies which salespeople are selling the complete package, which ones are doing a good job of defending their prices, and which ones have developed a profitable customer mix. Personally, I believe it's effective to rank each salesperson each month and offer incentives to the salesperson who earns the highest margin or shows the most improvement since the previous month.

Some retail computer systems include on this report the gross margins for each of the charge customers assigned to a particular salesperson. This feature makes this report especially strong as a management tool. Frequently, managers find that salespeople have become so close to a few customers that they let their relationship influence the prices they charge these accounts.

This report usually reveals that gross margins made by even floor salespeople will vary widely. Bear in mind that these are inside salespeople who are selling the same customers out of the same price book. However, the salespeople who are selling up, selling related items, and selling value will almost always generate the highest gross margins. When in the course of my consulting work I analyze the report on gross margin by salesperson, it's not at all unusual to see a spread of five percentage points between the gross margins generated by the best and the worst salespeople.

Gross margin by customer. Rarely do any two customers produce an identical gross margin. In fact, the differences between customers of like size, class, and sales volume often vary widely. No computerized report points out these inconsistencies better than this one.

Let's face it, some customers are better bargainers than others. Some buy a broader, more profitable mix of products. And some pay their bills more promptly than others. By identifying which customers' gross margins are acceptable and which aren't, managers and salespeople have additional tools to increase gross margins.

Here's an example: Refer to your accounts receivable aging report and jot down each customer who is in the 60-day column or beyond. Then pull out your report on gross margin by customer and jot down the gross margins your company is earning on each of the customers who don't pay their bills by their due date. If slow-pay customers aren't generating higher gross margins than prompt-pay accounts, there's an opportunity to inch up prices.

Forget for a second that the market usually allows you to earn higher gross margins on slow-pay accounts. They also cost more to maintain. So if you're not earning higher gross margins on slow-pay accounts, I believe you're leaving gross profit dollars on the table.

Major and minor category report. In order to get down to the real value of this report, it's necessary to do some "drilling." But first let me explain this report, in case you're not familiar with it. In a retail grocery store, a major category might be produce or pet foods. The minor category might be the various types of potatoes or, in the case of pet foods, it might be gourmet cat food. In a retail paint store, the major category might be stains and varnishes, and the minor category might be exterior finishes.

When setting up individual sku's in the inventory module, the software first asks which major category and then which minor category the sku will be a part of.

So in the case of paint, a manager would first analyze the major category report. Let's assume that he or she notices that the gross margin of the major category — paint — is somewhat lower this quarter than it was last quarter.

The next step would be to analyze each minor category, say, interior latex, enamel, exterior oil-based paints, etc., to determine which of the minor categories is pulling down the major category. Once the culprits among the minor categories are identified, the next step is to scrutinize each sku that makes up each of the minor categories in question. In each step in the process, the manager is looking for opportunities to increase gross margin.

Factor #19
PACKAGE SELLING

Some pricing strategists call this technique "bundling." It calls for a retailer to package several products together to reduce the incidence of "cherry-picking" by cost-conscious customers.

In sports, the objective is to create a level playing field; that is, make the physical attributes of the field, court, or ring exactly the same for the individuals or teams that are competing. The purpose, of course, is to make sure that the only difference between the competing teams is the quality of the players.

In business, the opposite is the case. In order to gain a competitive advantage, retailers do everything in their power to make the playing field as uneven as possible. They do their best to make it difficult for customers and prospects to make apples-to-apples comparisons. Package selling is one way to accomplish this.

It would be relatively easy for a customer to shop several retail stores and compare the prices being charged for a Gillette razor, for example. But if one retailer were to package razors, blades, and shaving cream together and price all three as a package, the comparison would be more difficult to make. The same idea would be effective if a customer were shopping around for a really good deal on a power saw. Imagine if one retailer were to not only offer power saws, but also packaged several different types of blades with the saw.

The definition of a commodity: "When the customer cannot discern any differences between the offerings of the various retailers."

Do you sell many of the same products as your competitors? And do your customers and prospects purchase these products frequently? If this is the case, your prices are most likely shopped more often, making the competitive price known for a wider group of products. The more aware customers are of market prices, the more they play one supplier against the others. If this sounds like your business, you know how difficult it is to differentiate yourself when you sell commodity-like products. To get out of the commodity rat race, it's critical that you make some alterations to your offering so that the playing field becomes less level.

Packaging several products together is one way not only to improve gross margins, but also to increase sales. I learned a lot about package selling from a professional speaker who sells self-improvement books and audiocassette and videocassette training tapes "in the back of the room" after his presentation. Members of the audience who want to hear or read more of what the speaker has to say are invited to purchase the educational products at the intermission. The books range in price from $10 to $30, and each cassette or cassette album is priced anywhere from $10 (for a single audiocassette) to $60 for a six-cassette album. Videocassettes start at $99 and go up to $299.

The speaker was averaging around $1,000 in product sales after each presentation. Then he heard about package selling from another speaker and decided to give the idea a try. Of course, he would sell single copies of his books and single cassettes or single albums, but he began to promote what he called value packs.

The value packs were composed of the same products he had been selling individually. The speaker used a clear plastic wrap to package the individual products.

Value Pack #1 contained two books, one video, and one audiocassette album and was offered at a 20% discount.

Value Pack #2 contained one book, one video, and two audiocassette albums and was offered at a 20% discount, as well.

Value Pack #3 contained two books, two videos, and three audiocassette albums and was offered at a 25% discount.

Value Pack #4 contained three books, three videos, three audiocassette albums, and two individual cassettes at a 30% discount.

Value Pack #5 contained every product the speaker had for sale: five books, four videos, five audiocassette albums, and four individual audiocassettes at a whopping 40% discount.

The value packs, along with individual unpackaged products, were stacked on a table in the back of the meeting room. After adding value packs, the speaker found his sales soared to an average of $3,400.

I asked the speaker why he thought the value pack idea caused sales to go up so much. "I believe it's because the Value Packs make it easier for the members of the audience to make a selection. We give them five choices, all at different price points and at different discounts."

"But what about your gross margin?" I asked. "Doesn't your margin take a beating?"

"Well, yes, my margins do suffer, but in my business I don't have any overhead to cover," he explained. "My costs are the same whether my product sales are $1,000 or $5,000. My focus is more on the total gross profit dollars I generate. And since most of the people in the audience will never hear me again, I have a very narrow window of selling opportunity. I have to get their attention while my presentation is still fresh in their minds."

The professional speaker in this example is a lot different from most of you who are reading this book in that, as he mentioned, he has no overhead. His cost for standing behind the table and selling product is no higher regardless of how much he sells. I cite this example because it was such a terrific success story for package selling.

One toothpaste company experienced sluggish sales and gross margins before it combined its toothpaste with dental floss, mouthwash, and a toothbrush into a travel kit as a package deal.

Computer companies offer packages regularly. An advertisement might read as follows: "Buy a computer and get a free keyboard, mouse, modem, and $1,000 worth of bundled software."

In a retail building supply business, dimension lumber — e.g., 2 x 4's, 2 x 6's, 2 x 8's — is a commodity product. If customers were buying just one piece of dimension lumber, perhaps the price wouldn't play such a big role in the customers' selection of a retailer, but customers often need dozens or hundreds of pieces of lumber and are motivated to do some shopping around.

Many successful building supply businesses around the country use package selling to "unlevel" the playing field when competing against The Home Depot and other discount retailers. Let's say you decide to add or replace a deck at the rear of your home. To prevent weather damage, you decide to use treated lumber. Here are the most likely steps you'd follow:

1. Measure the area you wish the deck to cover.

2. Call a contractor to look at your measurements and tell you how many of each size and length of lumber you'd need. You would also need to know what sizes of nails you'll need and how many nails of each size.

3. Once you have your materials list, you would visit a

number of building material stores to find which one had the best price.

When a customer has a materials list, it becomes awfully easy to "cherry pick" the various suppliers — that is, buy the 2 x 4's from the supplier with the lowest price on 2 x 4's, buy 4 x 4's from the suppler with the lowest prices on 4 x 4's, and so on.

Retailers that sell deck packages can eliminate much of this shopping and cherry picking. Deck packages are usually sold in specific sizes, such as 12' x 20', 15' x 30', and 14' x 25'. The package includes all the components necessary to complete the job. The only variable might be the height the deck will be built off the ground.

To further differentiate the deck offering from what the competition has, many retailers will add the labor and offer to sell the deck on an installed basis. This is frequently referred to as a turnkey job.

INSTALLED SALES

Varying forms of installed sales have enhanced the opportunities that retailers have to make package selling more appealing to customers. Any product that requires installation has the potential to be sold on an installed basis.

Computer retailers are improving their competitive position against large direct marketers by selling computers on an installed basis. Throw in a package that includes several hours of software training, and the discounter's bargain-basement prices are suddenly much less attractive.

Anytime you include a service — and training is a good example — in a package price, it makes the offering appear more valuable to the customer if a dollar value is attached to the service. Something like, "Four hours of training included — a value of $200 at full retail." Or, "Compare at

$50/hour." If you don't establish a value for the services you package with your products, the customer will think of them as a free offer. Anything that's free is perceived to be of little value.

Hardware retailers are selling storm doors, screen doors, window screens, hot water heaters, fireplaces, faucets, and even showerheads on an installed basis. They are also preassembling bicycles, lawn mowers, fertilizer spreaders, and wheelbarrows, and bundling the labor into the price of the product.

Toy retailers are jumping on the bandwagon when they assemble jungle gyms, swing sets, and bicycles. Nurseries aren't just selling plants anymore. For an additional fee, they'll come out and plant them for you.

Sam's Club sells automobile and truck tires, batteries, and other auto accessories at extremely competitive prices. So to compete, independent auto parts retailers offer installation packages to go along with the product. The same holds true for automobile headlights, brake lights, antennas, and radios.

There are several demographic factors that have caused installed sales to soar in popularity. North Americans appreciate their leisure time more than at any time in the past, so if a customer can afford to buy a product installed, the idea is very appealing. Another factor is the number of single parents in the workplace, women especially. After working a full-time job all day, picking up the kids at day care, preparing dinner, helping the kids with their homework, and putting them to bed, the last thing a single parent wants to do is pull out the toolbox and install a new plumbing kit in the commode tank.

Take a look at your product offering and identify the products that can be packaged with either accessory or complementary products or sold on an installed basis. Your gross margin will benefit.

Factor #20
SELLING SKILLS

When it comes to optimizing gross margin, there's no substitute for product knowledge. Customers are motivated to buy when they see a bargain, but especially when the purchase involves technology or a product the individual is uncomfortable with, there's usually a willingness to pay a little bit more up front to the retailer who has invested in knowledgeable personnel.

As the Fram oil filter folks say, "Pay me now or pay me later."

Everyone in retailing is familiar with the phrase, "knowledge is power." While the more customer contact personnel know about the products they sell the more effective they'll be at optimizing gross margin, product knowledge is not an end in and of itself. How many times have you been serviced by salespeople who possessed incredibly strong product knowledge, but lacked the verbal skills or the passion to effectively communicate what they know?

Sales skills are necessary to prevent customers from making a mistake. Have you ever made a purchase and after you used the product or service for a while wished that the salesperson had been just a little bit better? At least good enough to talk you into making a better decision?

Several months ago, my wife and I decided to purchase a pressure washer for our house at the beach. The area is extremely humid in the summer, and we began to notice a greenish mildew appearing on the sides of the house and on the deck. We were relatively new to the area, so to make the purchase, we visited a national chain with a store in Charleston, S.C. We were prepared to pay whatever was necessary to get a quality product that would last a long time.

When we walked into the store, I walked up to the service desk and asked where I would find pressure washers. "The paint department," a salesperson told me. "Walk down to aisle 3 and take a left. You can't miss it."

When I walked up to the paint counter, I asked a salesperson, "Who is the resident expert on pressure washers?"

"That would be Harold," she told me.

Harold had just mixed a gallon of paint and was taping the lid back on the can, so I waited until he was finished with his customer. I was next in line.

"Are you Harold?"

"Yes."

"Harold, I need to buy a pressure washer. Would you be kind enough to help me pick out a good one? Our house is about a 45-minute drive from here, so I want one that is reliable."

"Follow me," Harold said as he began walking slowly up the aisle.

When he arrived at the place where the pressure washers were located, he began reading aloud to me the information printed on the side of the box. "I can read, Harold. I need your expert advice."

"Well, if it were me," he said, "I'd go with this one. It operates at 3,000 PSI and should do the job you have in mind."

"Are you sure? My main concern is reliability. When I come down here to spend a few days away from the office, I don't want to have to spend my time running back and forth to Charleston to get this machine repaired."

"Yeah, it'll do a good job for you. My boss bought one just like it for himself."

When we got back to our house, I could hardly wait to hook up my new pressure washer and give it a test drive. It worked great. I must have used it for two hours in a row cleaning the concrete on our driveway. The next day, I decided to finish the driveway. But after I had used the pressure washer for about an hour, the hose blew out. Water was spraying everywhere.

The next day, I drove back to the store where I had made my purchase, but Harold had taken the day off. No one else in the store knew much about pressure washers, but I showed them which one I had bought. The problem was that they had no replacement hoses in stock. They recommended that I drive to another store in town that was sure to have a replacement hose. At that store I learned that the pressure washer I had bought came with a $1/4$" hose, and $3/8$" was standard.

"That hose you've got there is a piece of crap," the owner of the store told me. "I'm surprised it lasted as long as it did."

"How much will a $3/8$" hose cost me? I asked. "$90," he said without hesitation.

"Okay, I don't have any choice, but will this new one last me for a while?"

"Absolutely. It should last for years."

A few weeks later, I was using the pressure washer and the spray nozzle began to leak. A few minutes later it was leaking so badly that I had to quit and go back to the same man who had sold me the new $3/8$" hose.

"Look what happened to the spray nozzle," I told him. "Can it be repaired?"

"No way," he said. "How about coming back here into the shop and let me show you something?"

We walked back into his shop where he clamped the plastic spray nozzle into a vice and took it apart.

"See here," he said. "This nozzle is junk. One of the O rings is missing, too. No wonder it was leaking."

"How much will a new spray nozzle cost me?"

"I'll sell you a metal one that will last a long time, but it'll cost you another $90."

"What else do you think can go wrong with this spray washer?"

"There's only one more part that will probably go out on you," he said as he pointed to the part.

"And how much will that part cost me if and when it breaks?"

"Well, you might get lucky and not have to replace it for a while, but when it does go, it'll be another $90."

I later learned that the national chain I was doing business with had their pressure washers manufactured to their own specifications. The engine was excellent, but to keep their prices low, they had skimped on the hose and the nozzle.

I wish Harold had been a better salesperson. A more professional salesperson with greater product knowledge and more skills of persuasion would not have recommended that particular pressure washer to me. A true professional would have pointed out to me that, while the price of the product was reasonable, part of the reason was because the hose and the nozzle were of poor quality.

QUESTIONING SKILLS

Questioning is one of the most effective techniques to enhance a salesperson's professionalism. By asking customers and prospects well-designed, open-ended questions, the odds are excellent that the salesperson will find out just about everything he or she needs to know to not only make the sale, but to optimize gross margin, as well.

In my case, I am sometimes attracted not to the highest-quality clothes, but rather to those that are less expensive. I need to be reminded that I will usually get what I pay for when it comes to quality. And a quality garment will almost always be the best bargain because it will last longer and I will enjoy wearing it more.

Here are a few of the questions that a professional salesperson selling men's suits might ask a customer who has come into the store:

1. What kind of work do you do?

2. How often do you expect to wear this suit?

3. How many days in a row would you expect to wear the suit?

4. How much traveling do you do?

5. Do you travel in areas that experience extremes in temperature?

6. Do you spend a lot of time getting in and out of a car?

7. How much air travel do you do?

8. Will you be wearing this suit year-round?

9. How long do you generally expect a suit to last before it wears out?

10. How important to your success is your appearance?

11. Are you buying this suit for any particular occasion?

12. Do you have any particular preferences with regard to fabric?

Sales trainer Tony Alessandro makes this statement about the importance of asking good questions before making recommendations: "Offering a prescription without a proper diagnosis is malpractice."

What questions really do is give you the information you need to recommend the best product(s) and service(s) to fulfill the customer's needs.

TRAINING

One of the biggest obstacles to gaining a reputation for keeping a knowledgeable staff is training. The big question is how to best train your sales team so well that they are up to speed on the products and services you sell with respect to both product knowledge and sales skills.

Most retailers invite manufacturers' reps to periodically conduct product knowledge training programs with an emphasis on the products that each rep represents. Employee turnover, however, can mean that new employees may have missed out on some of the training sessions that took place before they came on board.

I know I have mentioned this before, but it needs to be repeated here. The best solution I've found to this problem is to videotape each training session. Be sure to tell the rep well in advance of the training session that you plan to videotape the program. Often, he or she will arrange for a senior executive or a product specialist to conduct the training. So this strategy will often guarantee you a more professional presentation.

After the videotaping is complete, be sure to assign an employee the responsibility for maintaining your library of videotapes. We also recommend that you make a duplicate copy immediately and use the duplicate for future training. This will reduce the odds that your original will be damaged or lost.

Factor #21
BE STINGY
WITH DISCOUNTS

Speaking of discounts, I'm reminded of what I once heard from a great entrepreneur from my home state of Georgia, Ely Callaway. (Ely Callaway passed away in 2001.)

Early in Ely's career, he was a management star at Burlington Industries, but the No. 1 position in the company did not seem to be in the cards for him. So rather than remain content with his position in the company, he left Burlington Industries and founded a wine company, Callaway Wines, in a growing region in California not known for the greatest grapes. But Ely Callaway knew wine.

Within four years of the founding of the winery, when the Queen of England toasted the United States on its bicentennial celebration, glasses all around were filled with Callaway wine.

Then another opportunity beckoned, and Ely Callaway transformed one more passion into a well-run enterprise, Callaway Golf. When asked how he engendered such great success in three disparate industries, Ely Callaway offered this advice:

"Produce a quality product, market it well, and never, never discount it."

I don't know about you, but I really enjoy getting a good

price when I make a major purchase. Remember that I said a "major purchase." That doesn't mean that I negotiate with the checkout clerk in the grocery store, but if I'm buying a piece of furniture, a suit of clothes, an automobile, or a lawn mower, I do my best to beat the asking price.

The best way I've found to be successful at getting the retailer to bend on price is to ask for a discount. There are all kinds of discounts in the retail world:

1. Volume discounts

2. Corporate discounts

3. Quantity discounts

4. Functional discounts

5. Professional discounts

6. New Year's discounts

7. End-of-month discounts

8. End-of-year discounts

9. Introductory discounts

10. Close-out discounts

11. Winter, spring, summer, and fall discounts

12. Anniversary discounts

13. Sale discounts

Do you remember the story I told back in Chapter 10 about my experience in the furniture store with my wife? In that story, the store owner very willingly and unnecessarily offered me a 15% discount if I purchased both the armoire and the pencil post bed.

In my seminars, I encourage owners, managers, and salespeople — anyone who has pricing authority — to memorize effective responses to routine customer attempts to receive a discount. Here are a few responses my seminar attendees have suggested that the owner of the furniture store might have offered to avoid giving me a discount and still have gotten the sale:

1. "Sorry, Mr. Lee, we can't discount these items."

Good answer, but remember, the saleswoman had already let the cat out of the bag that the owner could and would discount.

2. "Mr. Lee, we would really like to have your business, but we've already discounted those two pieces of furniture as much as we can."

I like this response. In a nice way, the owner is telling the customer — even though she really wants his business — that she can't do any better.

3. "We can discount the pencil post bed, but we can't discount the armoire."

I see the point that the seminar attendee is trying to make. This is an attempt to split the difference, so to speak. But the owner wouldn't be wise to give in this easily.

4. "I don't know, Mr. Lee. That armoire has been a pretty popular piece of furniture ever since we got it in. I'm not sure, but I seem to remember that someone was coming back this afternoon to make a decision on it."

I don't know if the owner is telling the truth about someone coming in to make a decision, but a statement like that would certainly cause my negotiating mood to disappear. Remember, I really have no choice; I can't afford to lose the only armoire in the world that will fit that narrow opening. And last but not least, I don't want to offend my wife!

5. *"We don't mind discounting items in our inventory that we're trying to move out, but these two pieces of furniture are relatively new. If you'll check with me in a couple of months — and if they're still here then — I'll be happy to discuss a discount with you."*

Another good answer. I especially like it because it's a polite way of saying no.

ARE YOU A DEALER OR RETAILER?

Dealer: Someone who engages in trading or bargaining.
Retailer: Someone who sells goods to customers.

So, is your business engaged in trading and bargaining, or is it engaged in selling? I believe most of the readers of this book will fall under the umbrella of retailer as opposed to dealer.

When I think of a dealer, I most often think of an automobile dealer. Most of us hate to buy cars because of the way automobile dealers approach their profession. No matter how good a price you negotiate for an automobile, you can always find someone who paid less for the same make, same model, with the same accessories. Buying a new car is a less than enjoyable experience for most of us because we never believe we can trust the automobile salesperson.

A few years ago, I bought a car for my wife. Here's the way the transaction went after I walked onto the BMW used-car lot.

"How much are you asking for the black two-door out there?" I said as I pointed to a six-year-old BMW with 43,000 miles.

"Why don't you make me an offer?" the salesperson responded.

I had prepared myself for the ordeal of buying this car by going to my bank and getting a copy of the latest edition of the little NADA book that gives a rough estimate of how much cars are worth at both wholesale and retail. Most importantly, it also reveals the loan value of the car.

"Please, let's not approach the transaction this way," I pleaded. "I have my checkbook here in my hand. I've already talked to my banker about how much she'll loan me on the car. If you'll just tell me how much you're asking for the car, I'll either write you a check or I'll just pass."

"Mr. Lee, what's the car worth to you? If you'll make me an offer, I'll take the deal to my sales manager and see if he'll take it or not."

If my wife had not had her heart set on that particular car, I would have politely gotten up and walked out, but after looking at dozens of cars, this was the one she wanted.

"OK, it appears that I can't buy a car here the way I want to buy it. I guess you're telling me I have to buy it your way. Is that right?"

"Well, I do need for you to make me an offer, Mr. Lee."

"So you want to negotiate the price. Is that what you're saying?"

"If you'll make me an offer, I'll go to bat for you with my sales manager. I really want you to have this car."

"I don't like this. You know what you paid for the BMW I want to buy. You have been servicing my wife's old BMW for five years, so you know the service record on my trade-in like the back of your hand. You also know what my trade-in is worth. I'm not in the car business. But since I have no choice, here's what I'm willing to pay, based on the information in the NADA book. Full retail is listed at $28,400 and wholesale is listed at $22,100. From all I read, dealerships earn an average of 12% mark-up on used cars.

Assuming that you paid wholesale for the car, I'll give you wholesale plus 12%, which comes to $24,752."

"You know, Mr. Lee, we don't use that little yellow book here. We use a black book."

"Well, regardless of what color your book is, my banker told me that she uses the yellow NADA book to determine how much she'll loan me on the car. So please go ahead and talk to your sales manager. I'm in a hurry. I need to get back to work."

The salesman wrote $24,752 on the sales contract and left me sitting in his office for about five minutes while he walked next door to speak to the sales manager about my offer. I could see the two of them talking through the window that partitioned the two offices. Finally, he walked back into his office with a big smile on his face. He pulled out a piece of paper and started writing.

"Mr. Lee, my sales manager says that there's no way he can let that car go for $24,752. That's below the price we paid for the car. Here's what he says he'll take."

The salesman wrote $26,900 on the piece of paper.

"I'm sorry, but it looks as if we can't do business," I said as I got up to leave.

"Wait a minute, Mr. Lee, just make me a counter-offer and let me take another crack at my sales manager."

This time I told him that I'd pay $25,000 maximum for the car, and that that was my final offer.

The salesman left again and stepped back across the hall to the sales manager's office. They talked for another five minutes. When he returned, he wrote $25,900 on the slip of paper. "How does this look?" he asked.

I stood up again. "I told you $25,000 was the maximum I'd pay."

As I moved toward the door, the salesman stopped me and asked me if I would agree to allow him to approach his sales manager just one more time. I said that that would be fine with me.

When he came back, he said, "Mr. Lee, you've just bought yourself a car. And by the way, my sales manager says that you got yourself a really good deal."

I signed the paperwork and drove away.

How many consumers enjoy doing business this way? Am I alone in my disdain for wheeling and dealing with a less-than-professional car salesperson? Based on the comments I have received from seminar audiences when we've discussed buying a car, I believe I have a lot of company.

Perhaps this is why so many consumers are beating a path to the doors of Saturn and Lexus, two organizations that have made the switch from "dealing" to the profession of "retailing" the cars they sell.

My company was retained by a heating and air conditioning retailer to help improve its gross margin. Once I got into the assignment, I found that not only the manager, but every salesperson in the store was authorized to negotiate any price they felt would get the business. Their customers had learned that if they wanted a better price, all they had to do was ask for it.

During interviews with the salespeople, I quickly learned that very few of them had the courage to say no when they were asked to discount the prices that appeared in the price book. Customers were successfully using the "flinch" to intimidate the sales force. *(See Chapter 10 on dealing with pricing objections.)*

Is your company a dealer or a retailer? The great majority of my clients call themselves retailers (some of my larger clients call themselves distributors), but when it comes to discounting, they quite often behave more like dealers.

I was called in to perform a business audit for a hardware retailer in south Georgia. After we began our interviews, it became pretty obvious that more customers received discounts than paid the price marked on the product.

"It's always been this way here," one counter salesperson told us.

"Our customers expect it," said another.

"If we didn't discount, we'd lose half our business to the competition," said still another.

Caution: I always caution my clients to resist the temptation to negotiate too large a percentage of their sales transactions. Salespeople have the tendency to blame price when they lose an order, but the truth is that salespeople who lose orders are more likely to be outsold than they are outpriced.

Rule: If you do decide to give your salespeople pricing authority, don't neglect to give them some training in negotiating skills. Another good rule is to tie their compensation plan to the gross margin they achieve. *(See Chapter 25 on gross margin-based incentive plans.)*

Factor #22
MARK-UP VERSUS
GROSS MARGIN

Make sure all of your salespeople and buyers understand the difference between mark-up on cost and gross profit margin.

Most managers take for granted that retail employees who have been around the business for several years understand the difference between mark-up and gross margin, but nothing could be further from the truth.

This point was brought home to me several years ago when I was conducting a sales seminar in eastern North Carolina. I had spent quite a bit of time that day emphasizing the difference between mark-up on cost and gross profit margin. When I called for a coffee break, a veteran road salesperson asked if he could speak to me privately in his office.

I'm not sure of this salesperson's exact age, but from his appearance I assumed that he was well into his 50s. And he had been selling for most of his adult life.

"Mr. Lee," he said to me agitatedly, "I didn't want to say anything in front of the group, but I'm totally confused over what you're saying about mark-up versus gross margin."

"OK," I said, "how can I help?"

"Well, let me put it in the form of a question. Let's say that I have an item here that costs me $100. OK?"

"OK."

"Now, I mark it up 50% and sell it for $150. OK?"

"OK," I said as I nodded my head.

"I made $50, right?"

"Right."

"Now, in that seminar you're conducting out there, you're telling us that when we buy an item for $100 and sell it for $150 that we're only earning a 33 $1/3$% gross margin. Am I correct?"

"Yes, you're correct," I answered.

"Well, that's what's got me confused. What exactly happened to my $50 profit?"

"Look at it this way," I said. "Nothing happened to your $50 profit. It's just a matter of what you divide the $50 by. If you divide it by your cost; that is, by $100, you get 50%, which is your mark-up. But if you divide the $50 by the price you sold the item for; that is, $150, you get 33 $1/3$%, or your gross margin.

"Gross profit divided by cost equals mark-up on cost, but gross profit divided by sell price equals gross margin. You earn $50 in gross profit both ways."

"So if I make $50 regardless of how I arrive at it, what difference does it make?"

"Good question," I answered. "Every expense item in a business is measured on the basis of its relationship to sales. For example, if I were conducting a consulting assignment for your general manager, I would look at the store's salaries as a percentage of sales. I would also look at insurance expense, interest expense, and benefits as a percentage of sales. By looking at businesses' expenses as a percentage of sales, companies' success levels can be compared even though the sizes of the respective businesses may vary. So with that in mind, it would be pretty inconsistent if you looked at every expense item in the business as a percentage of sales, but looked at gross profit as a percentage of cost. This would not be comparing apples to apples."

"Okay, the lightbulb just went off," he said. "Thank you for taking the time to explain why looking at gross profit as a percentage of sales versus a percentage of cost is so important."

The reason it's so important for personnel involved in pricing to grasp the critical difference between mark-up and gross margin, is because they so frequently lull themselves into believing that they are earning a satisfactory gross margin, but all along they have gotten the two confused.

Factor #23
APPLES-TO-APPLES COMPARISONS

Analyze each competitive quote or bid to make sure you are comparing apples to apples. Especially when customers are purchasing a relatively large quantity of materials, there's a tendency for them to look only at the bottom line of the quotations they get. Few customers are conscientious enough to thoroughly analyze the specific products and quantities that make up each bid.

This point was quite vividly impressed upon me while working with a Sacramento-based retailer that was required to bid on just about all of the material the company sold. In an attempt to do a better job of making apples-to-apples comparisons, the owner created a process he named Bidworks. There was nothing particularly unique about Bidworks. It was the process of meticulously analyzing each competitive bid and comparing that bid against his own bid that made Bidworks so effective.

In the time I spent with this client, I saw the owner compare dozens of bids, and never once did I see identical products and identical quantities make up any two bids. They were all different. The following are some of the differences I observed:

1. Different brand names were often substituted for those specified.

2. Different grades were substituted.

3. Although identical items were quoted, the quantities were different.

4. Different sizes.

But here's what I found to be most interesting: If a supplier listed a special order product but failed to bid on it, a zero appeared in the price column. So the supplier that did take the time to locate the product and bid on it was automatically at a disadvantage if the customer merely looked at the bottom line of the respective bids.

To reduce the time necessary to prepare a quotation from scratch, it's a common practice for a salesperson to convince a customer to remove the prices from a competitor's bid and then hand over a copy of the material list for him or her to price.

DIRTY TRICK, OR EFFECTIVE TECHNIQUE?

Because the dollar value of the total bid is the basis most customers use to determine who will receive the order, one of my clients shared with me a technique he used to prevent competitors from using his hard work to their advantage. He would prepare a legitimate bid, but before he would hand it to the customer, he would increase the quantities of material by 10%. Therefore when the customer went to his competitor for a comparative bid and the competitor priced his bid — even if the prices were identical — their prices would be 10% higher than his because they were pricing a greater quantity of merchandise.

So in this case, even though the customer makes sure he or she is comparing apples to apples, he or she may still not be aware that the quantities to do the job are inflated.

Incidentally, I asked this client what he would do if his customer tried to force him to deliver the inflated quantities he had included on his bid. His answer was this: "That's never been a problem with my customers. All I'm obligated to do is supply enough materials to complete the job. If my competitor is going to be lazy enough to simply use my material take-off and my quantities, he's going to get burned."

In my industry — retail building supplies — one of the most effective tactics category killers like Atlanta-based The Home Depot and Minneapolis-based Menard's use to generate consumer traffic is a special deal on premium windows. The deal is called 40-40-40, which stands for:

1. 40% off list price.

2. 40% down payment.

3. 40 days for delivery.

This discounted price structure wouldn't be so devastating to local independently owned retail window merchants except that customers visit an independently owned store to take advantage of their salespeople's technical expertise. While large discount stores may have some pretty appealing prices on windows, they frequently don't have the in-house technical expertise to figure out what size each of the windows needs to be to fit the rough openings.

So after getting the independent merchant's personnel to analyze their house plans and specify the manufacturer's product numbers, prospective customers would tell the salesperson that they needed a little while to think about their purchase and would be back in touch soon. Of course their plan all along was to take the material take-off prepared by the independently owned merchant back to the discount store and buy the product there at a lower price.

While such a buying tactic is hardly fair to the independent merchant, some customers don't allow business ethics to get in the way of saving money. To level the playing field, several local retailers who quickly became fed up with being abused by so many customers decided to fight fire with fire. When the customer would come in to get window sizes specified from an analysis of their house plans, the salesperson would "accidentally on purpose" jot down several windows with the wrong item numbers. If the customer came back to the local merchant and bought the product there, the salesperson would correct the error, but if the customer took the material list to the discount store, the salesperson there who had insufficient product knowledge to recognize the mistake would order the wrong windows.

This trick is designed to send a message to local consumers who take free product knowledge from one merchant and do business with another. The only problem with this tactic is that it causes the customers so much inconvenience. But then again, think of the hours of effort that the technically competent salesperson spent figuring out which was the right window for each opening.

Factor #24
DIRECT SALES,
EMPLOYEE SALES,
INTER-COMPANY SALES

All three of these classifications of sales usually carry lower gross margins than those of regular sales.

Direct sales. Many companies take advantage of the cost savings, especially on large orders, by asking the manufacturer to ship the material directly to the end user. Because other suppliers may be using the same direct-sales technique, a sale such as this can become highly competitive. So the gross margin on direct sales is usually substantially lower than what would be possible on material that's shipped out of the company's on-hand inventory.

Employee sales. Many companies offer employees a substantial employee discount on merchandise they purchase for themselves or their immediate family.

Inter-company sales. This category encompasses material that is transferred between branches of the same company; it's usually priced either at cost or at a standard mark-up or gross margin that's less than that for material sold to the company's regular customer base.

There's certainly nothing wrong with the above pricing practices, but they must be carefully monitored. Special employee pricing is especially likely to be abused. Unscrupulous employees sometimes purchase goods, charge them to their own account, then turn around and sell the merchandise to friends or neighbors at a profit. Or they purchase material for friends and family members who are not supposed to get employee pricing.

Employee purchases should be monitored monthly and scrutinized when irregularities are spotted. I believe all companies should make it a policy that abusing the employee discount policy is grounds for termination.

When inter-company sales and direct sales are inter-mingled on the income statement (P&L) with sales that earn more normal gross margins, gross margin is bound to be distorted. The higher the proportion of low-margin direct, employee, and inter-company sales to regular sales, the greater the distortion. When these conditions do occur, managers may become unnecessarily alarmed when they see their gross margin for the month take a sudden dive.

To prevent distortions, I recommend that my clients set up their accounting systems so that inter-company sales and direct sales are not intermingled with regular sales that earn normal gross margins.

One procedure that many companies use is to capture the gross profit on these kinds of sales under other income and avoid running these special sales classifications through regular sales. This practice allows managers to compare each class of sale against established standards.

Gross margin is difficult enough to manage, so always make every attempt to remove all the distortions you can identify.

Factor #25
GROSS MARGIN-BASED INCENTIVE PLANS

Managers, salespeople, and support personnel are first of all human beings. Some are lazy. Some possess an incredible work ethic. Some are more ambitious than others. But there's one thing all workers will respond to: An opportunity to earn more money. I know that I've always enjoyed being in control — at least to some extent — of my economic destiny.

In the management seminars I conduct, I am quick to point out that incentive compensation plans are no substitute for proven management techniques. I learned this lesson the hard way. I used to believe that all I had to do was put the right incentive plan in place and I wouldn't have to manage. I was wrong. But one thing is for sure: Well-designed incentive pay plans do help get workers' attention and help them focus.

In 1965, I left my home state of Georgia and moved my family to Mobile, Ala., where I became a sales representative for the Ruberoid Co. (now GAF Corp.). I was paid a straight commission to sell roofing, siding, and insulation products to commercial customers.

If I remember correctly, our commission on most products averaged about 1 percent of sales. However, on our highly profitable siding products, our commission soared to 5 percent of sales. The only problem was that in the Deep South, few home builders used our siding products, so just about the only sales we made were for repairs or additions to homes where our siding was already installed.

But regardless of the higher commission structure, I learned from my veteran colleagues that I was wasting my time trying to sell siding. I was convinced that my time was best spent selling products that had less customer resistance.

Then one day in the mail, I received a memo that explained that for the next three months, the company was paying a special incentive of $1 per unit of siding that we sold. Wow! They called it a "spiff." I had never heard of a spiff before, but the idea of earning such a large incentive over and above my commission got my attention. And to take advantage of our competitive spirit, the company offered a special prize to the sales representative who sold the most units of siding during the promotion.

I got busy and developed a personal strategy for selling siding. I was a young and inexperienced salesperson, so my strategy was not very complex. But it did get results. Each time I visited a building supply dealer or commercial siding contractor, I explained that my company was conducting a contest that I was determined to win. I asked if the customer would agree to allow me to topload two pallets (one pallet each of two popular designs) along with the roofing products they were ordering.

It worked!

Just about every customer I visited agreed to help me out. I didn't win the contest, but I did receive a special spiff check for more than $400, not too shabby for a 23-year-old sales rep in 1965.

PAY COMMISSIONS ON GROSS PROFIT, NOT SALES

I don't know about your industry, but in most of the businesses I have worked with, the products that carry the lowest gross margins are usually the easiest to sell. Therefore, the products that carry the highest gross margins are the most difficult and time-consuming to sell.

To make it easier for managers to motivate salespeople to spend the necessary time to promote and sell higher-margin products, I've found that it's effective to pay sales commissions on an escalating scale that varies with the percentage of gross margin they generate each month. Figure 5 *(see next page)* illustrates such a plan.

One of the basic rules when designing a compensation plan is to make it simple. Some compensation consultants say the company's compensation plan should be so simple that it can be written on the back of an envelope.

I like this particular plan because I believe most salespeople find it easier to calculate their commission when it's based on a percentage of sales. However, by tying the sales commission to gross margin, salespeople receive a greater monthly reward when they're able to achieve a higher monthly gross margin. An alternative, just as effective, is to pay a higher commission on product categories that generate higher gross margins.

Figure 5. Sales Commission Plan Tied to Gross Margin

Monthly Gross Margin Achieved	Percentage of Gross Profit
Below 16.00%..	Negotiable
16.0 - 16.99%..	10.0%
17.0 - 17.99%..	10.5%
18.0 - 18.99%..	11.0%
19.0 - 19.99%..	11.5%
20.0 - 20.99%..	12.0%
21.0 - 21.99%..	12.5%
22.0 - 22.99%..	13.0%
23.0 - 23.99%..	13.5%
24.0 - 24.99%..	14.0%
25.0 - 25.99%..	14.5%
26.0 - 26.99%..	15.0%
All above 27%..	15.5%

Monthly Gross Margin Achieved	Percentage of Sales
Below 13%	Negotiable
13.0 - 13.99%..	1.0%
14.0 - 14.99%..	1.1%
15.0 - 15.99%..	1.2%
16.0 - 16.99%..	1.3%
17.0 - 17.99%..	1.4%
18.0 - 18.99%..	1.5%
19.0 - 19.99%..	1.6%
20.0 - 20.99%..	1.7%
21.0 - 21.99%..	1.8%
22.0 - 22.99%..	1.9%
23.0 - 23.99%..	2.0%
24.0 - 24.99%..	2.2%
25.0 - 25.99%..	2.4%
26.0 - 26.99%..	2.6%
All above 27%..	2.8%

All industries have some product categories that are more profitable than others. In the building supply industry, the list below shows product categories at one of my client's businesses, ranked from the lowest gross margin to the highest:

1. Framing products, including sheathing, plywood, OSB, dimension lumber

2. Engineered wood, such as glulams and I-beams

3. Windows

4. Doors

5. Hardware

6. Millwork, including interior and exterior trim

7. Custom millwork, such as custom-made cabinets and entrance doors

Factor #26
ESTABLISH PROCEDURES
TO PREVENT ERRORS;
MISTAKES LEAD
TO MARKDOWNS

Management and sales personnel in most of the retail businesses I have worked with do an outstanding job of putting out fires and solving problems. They do a less than sterling job, however, of preventing problems from occurring in the first place.

In today's highly competitive retail environment, customers demand a retail policy of 100% customer satisfaction. Even when it's the customer's fault, it's still the retailer who must eat many mistakes. Retailers who have yet to figure this out won't survive long, so retailers must spend more time on preventive measures.

Here are a couple of examples of how small procedural changes can save your company precious gross profit dollars:

1. In many retail businesses, special orders — products the retail store doesn't carry in stock but will special order for the customer — make up roughly 20% of total sales. Special-order merchandise is usually not as price-sensitive

as stock merchandise and therefore provides an excellent opportunity to enhance gross margins.

One frequent problem, however, is when the special-order item arrives from the manufacturer or distributor and the customer refuses — for whatever reason — to accept the item. Sometimes customers have changed their minds or have grown impatient and bought a substitute product from a competitor. Regardless, the retailer is stuck with special merchandise that often cannot be returned.

Another common problem is that the salesperson and the customer miscommunicate. The product that arrives is not the product the customer wanted.

Possible solutions:

To help prevent problem number one, charge the customer a 50% deposit or, if possible, ask the customer to pay for the item in full before agreeing to special order it from a supplier.

To help prevent problem number two, it's a good idea to write up the special-order sale on a specially designed form that provides space for the customer's signature. Make sure this form is imprinted with a special clause that reads:

The undersigned certifies that he/she has read the description of the item he/she is special ordering and agrees that its specifications are correct.

2. Sometimes no one is available to sign for merchandise that's delivered to the customer. This is a common problem among retailers who deliver. Sometimes a dishonest customer claims the merchandise was never received, but, more often, the merchandise may have been stolen.

One of my clients came up with a great way to help prevent this problem: The client assigned a digital camera to each delivery vehicle. When drivers made a delivery, they would take a snapshot of the material sitting on the customer's jobsite, loading dock, etc. If the customer did question that the delivery was made or made accurately, the supplier was able to produce proof of delivery via a photograph.

Try this: Keep good records and identify the mistakes and errors that make up approximately 80% of the snafus that occur in your business. (While it would be ideal to identify 100% of mistakes and errors, it is also impractical. The 80/20 rule usually applies.) Then, one by one, sit down with your people and brainstorm what you might do to prevent each of the frequently occurring mistakes you've identified from recurring.

KNOWLEDGE IS POWER

The better all employees understand the factors affecting gross profit margin, the more effectively they can control them. We encourage our clients to hold in-house gross margin control brainstorming sessions. See how many factors your own personnel can add to this list.

APPENDIX

GROSS MARGINS OF SELECTED RETAIL COMPANIES

AUTOMOBILE DEALERS

Company	Sales (000)	GPM	Op. Margin	Net A/T
Auto Nation ('01)	$19,989,300	14.4%	2.5%	1.2%
Asbury Auto. ('01)	$4,318,300	15.6%	2.9%	1.0%
CarMax ('02)	$3,201,700	12.06%	4.6%	2.8%
Group 1 Auto. ('01)	$3,996,400	15.2%	3.3%	1.4%
Sonic Auto.('01)	$6,337,400	15.4%	3.2%	1.3%
United Auto ('01)	$6,220,700	14.2%	2.5%	.7%

AUTO PARTS STORES

Company	Sales (000)	GPM	Op. Margin	Net A/T
Advanced ('01)	$2,517,600	42.4%	3.5%	.5%
Auto Zone ('01)	$4,818,200	44.5%	10.7%	3.6%
Genuine Parts ('01)	$8,220,700	31.7%	6.9%	3.6%
Pep Boys ('02)	$2,183,700	32.2%	4.7%	1.6%

BOOKSTORES

Company	Sales (000)	GPM	Op. Margin	Net A/T
Barnes & Noble('02)	$4,870,400	27.0%	5.1%	1.3%
Borders ('02)	$3,387,900	30.8%	5.8%	2.6%
Books-A-Million('02)	$442,900	26.7%	2.4%	.9%

DEPARTMENT STORES

Company	Sales (000)	GPM	Op. Margin	Net A/T
Belk ('02)	$2,243,200	31.7%	6.1%	2.8
Dillard's ('02)	$8,154,900	32.5%	.9%	.9%
Federated ('02)	$15,651,000	43.5%	8.4%	(Loss)
J.C. Penney ('02)	$32,004,000	28.4%	2.0%	.3%
Lord & Taylor	*(See May Department Stores)*			
May Dept. Strs('02)	$14,175,000	35.0%	10.5%	5.0%
Neiman Marcus('01)	$3,015,500	35.6%	6.7%	3.6%
Nordstrom ('02)	$5,634,100	36.9%	2.6%	2.2%
Saks Fifth Ave. ('02)	$6,070,600	34.8%	2.3%	.4%
Sears ('02)	$41,078,000	35.6%	8.9%	1.8%
Stein Mart ('02)	$1,320,000	25.3%	1.3%	1.2%
Syms ('02)	$287,700	33.7%	(Loss)	(Loss)
Value City ('02)	$2,283,900	39.9%	(Loss)	(Loss)

DISCOUNT RETAILERS

Company	Sales (000)	GPM	Op. Margin	Net A/T
Ames ('02)	$3,254,000	25.1%	(Loss)	(Loss)
Best Buy ('02)	$19,597,600	24.2%	4.8%	2.9%
Big Lots ('02)	$3,433,300	41.1%	(Loss)	(Loss)
Burlington Coat('01)	$2,400,300	34.7%	3.6%	3.0%
Costco ('01)	$34,797,000	12.9%	2.9%	1.7%
Cost Plus ('02)	$568,500	37.3%	6.0%	3.6%
Dollar General ('02)	$5,322,900	30.7%	7.0%	3.9%

Gross Margin

Company	Sales (000)	GPM	Op. Margin	Net A/T
Dollar Tree ('01)	$1,987,300	36.0%	10.3%	6.2%
Family Dollar ('01)	$3,665,400	35.3%	8.1%	5.2%
Friedman's Jlrs. ('01)	$411,000	47.4%	4.8%	3.0%
Goody's ('02)	$1,192,500	26.9%	(Loss)	(Loss)
Kohl's ('02)	$7,488,700	34.4%	11.4%	6.6%
K-Mart ('02)	$36,151,000	19.5%	(Loss)	(Loss)
99 Cents Only ('01)	$578,300	39.4%	12.8%	8.4%
Ross Stores ('02)	$2,986,600	31.1%	8.6%	5.2%
Signet Jewelry('01)	$1,028,200	18.7%	12.9%	8.0%
Stein Mart ('02)	$1,320,200	25.3%	1.1%	1.2%
Target ('02)	$39,888,000	31.7%	6.7%	3.4%
TJX Cos. ('02)	$10,709,000	26.1%	8.4%	4.7%
Wal-Mart ('02)	$217,799,000	22.7%	4.6%	3.1%

DRUGSTORES

Company	Sales (000)	GPM	Op. Margin	Net A/T
CVS Corp. ('01)	$22,241,400	25.6%	5.7%	1.9%
Eckerd	(Subsidiary of J.C. Penney)			
Longs Drug ('02)	$4,304,700	27.5%	2.1%	1.1%
Phar-Mor ('01)	$1,241,000	17.2%	(Loss)	(Loss)
Rite Aid ('02)	$15,171,100	24.8%	.3%	Loss
Walgreens ('01)	$24,623,000	17.8%	5.7%	1.9%

EYE CARE RETAILERS

Company	Sales (000)	GPM	Op. Margin	Net A/T
Cole Vision ('02)	$1,101,300	70.1%	3.1%	.5%
Eye Care Ctrs. ('01)	$336,000	68.9%	5.9%	(Loss)
U.S. Vision ('02)	$134,800	69.9%	5.9%	(Loss)

FAST FOOD RETAILERS

Company	Sales (000)	GPM	Op. Margin	Net A/T
Jack in the Box ('01)	$1,833,600	22.9%	8.4%	4.5%
McDonald's ('01)	$14,870,000	57.5%	19.5%	11.0%
Steak N Shake ('01)	$448,700	27.5%	8.1%	4.9%
Wendy's ('01)	$2,391,200	28.0%	13.8%	8.1%

FOOD CONVENIENCE STORES

Company	Sales (000)	GPM	Op. Margin	Net A/T
Dairy Mart ('02)	$646,900	20.6%	(Loss)	(Loss)
Ito-Yokado ('01) *(7-Eleven)*	$26,440,000	33.9%	5.3%	1.6%
The Pantry ('01)	$2,643,000	18.4%	2.3%	(Loss)
Uni-Marts ('01)	$420,400	21.0%	1.6%	.1%

GROCERY RETAILERS

Company	Sales (000)	GPM	Op. Margin	Net A/T
A & P ('02)	$10,973,300	31.1%	(Loss)	(Loss)
Albertson's ('02)	$37,931,000	31.1%	4.5%	1.3%
Delhaize Amer. ('01)	$14,913,200	25.4%	4.3%	1.1%
Harris Teeter ('01) *(Ruddick Corp.)*	$2,743,300	30.6%	3.5%	(Loss)
Ingle's ('01)	$1,943,400	28.4%	2.9%	.9%
Kroger ('02)	$50,098,000	27.3%	5.0%	2.1%
Pathmark ('02)	$3,963,300	28.0%	(Loss)	(Loss)
Publix ('01)	$15,370,000	26.5%	5.0%	3.5%
Safeway ('01)	$34,301,000	33.3%	7.5%	3.7%
Shoprite ('01)	$820,600	24.5%	2.3%	1.1%
Weis Markets ('01) *(also Superpetz stores)*	$1,988,200	29.3%	3.2%	2.5%
Winn-Dixie ('02)	$12,334,400	29.1%	3.0%	.7%

Gross Margin

HOME CENTERS

Company	Sales (000)	GPM	Op. Margin	Net A/T
BMC-West ('01)	$1,092,900	29.9%	3.8%	1.9%
Home Depot ('02)	$53,553,000	31.6%	9.2%	5.7%
Lowe's Cos. ('02)	$22.111,100	28.8%	8.0%	1.9%
Wickes Lbr. ('01)	$1,001,000	21.5%	10.5%	(Loss)
Wolohan ('01)	$239,800	24.2%	0.6%	2.0%

OFFICE SUPPLY STORES

Company	Sales (000)	GPM	Op. Margin	Net A/T
Buhrmann ('01)	$9,276,000	21.3%	3.3%	.5%
Office Depot ('01)	$11,154,100	30.1%	3.3%	1.8%
Office Max ('02)	$4,636,000	25.5%	(Loss)	(Loss)
Staples ('02)	$10,744,400	26.2%	4.7%	2.5%

SPECIALTY RETAILERS

Company	Sales (000)	GPM	Op. Margin	Net A/T
Ann Taylor ('02)	$1,299,600	53.3%	4.6%	2.2%
Bed, Bath & B.('02)	$2,928,700	43.4%	11.8%	7.5%
Benneton ('01)	$869,600	44.9%	21.4%	7.1%
Bombay Co. ('02)	$437,000	32.1%	6.4%	.8%
Chico's ('02)	$378,100	59.4%	17.9%	11.2%
Charming Shoppes ('02)	$1,993,800	30.0%	2.4%	Loss
Circuit City ('02)	$9,589,800	24.3%	2.2%	2.0%
Donna Karan ('00)	$662,700	32.9%	3.7%	2.9%
Galyans ('02)	$482,500	33.1%	5.5%	1.0%
Gap ('02)	$13,847,900	35.8%	2.4%	(Loss)
Haverty's ('01)	$678,100	50.7%	5.2%	3.3%
Intimate Brands('01)	$5,117,200	42.3%	14.7%	8.5%
J. Crew ('02)	$777,900	40.6%	2.6%	(Loss)
Land's End ('02)	$1,569,100	45.6%	7.2%	4.3%

Lillian Vernon ('02)	$259,600	42.7%	(Loss)	(Loss)
The Limited ('02)	$9,363,000	37.7%	8.0%	5.5%
Linens 'N Things('01)	$1,823,800	42.9%	5.0%	1.6%
Liz Claiborne ('02)	$3,448,500	44.3%	10.1%	5.6%
Men's Wearhouse ('02)	$1,273,200	38.7%	5.8%	3.4%
Pier One ('01)	$1,411,500	39.1%	10.7%	6.7%
Natl. Record Mart ('01)	$125,900	36.4%	(Loss)	(Loss)
Petco ('01)	$1,151,200	29.0%	1.2%	(Loss)
PetSmart ('02)	$2,501,000	30.7%	2.8%	1.6%
Restoration Hdwr. ('02)	$366,500	27.0%	(Loss)	(Loss)
Spiegel ('00)	$3,724,800	49.3%	7.3%	3.5%
Sports Authority ('02)	$1,415,600	30.3%	1.8%	.9%
Talbots ('02)	$1,612,500	43.3%	13.0%	7.9%
Tiffany ('02)	$1,606,500	62.8%	19.3%	10.8%
Toys R Us ('02)	$11,019,000	31.0%	3.2%	.6%
Wms.-Sonoma('02)	$2,086,700	41.5%	6.1%	3.6%

RECOMMENDED READING LIST FOR NEGOTIATING BASICS

How to Sell at Prices Higher than your Competitors, by Larry Steinmetz, Ph.D. 800-323-2835. Publisher: Horizon Publications Inc., Boulder, CO. Cost: $24.95. Visit *www.pricingexpert.com.*

Secrets of Power Negotiating, by Roger Dawson. Cost: $11.19 plus shipping and handling, at Amazon.com.

Give & Take, by Chester L. Karrass. Publisher: Thomas Y. Crowell Co.

The Negotiating Game: How to Get What You Want, by Chester L. Karrass.

For $21.70 plus S&H, buy both *Give & Take* and *The Negotiating Game* from Amazon.com.

How to Negotiate High Profit Sales, by Bob Gibson. One audio-cassette. Cost: $27.95 plus S&H. Phone 415-331-8808. Visit *bgibson@negotiationresources.com* for information about Gibson's Train the Trainer Video presentation for sales managers.

The Haggler's Handbook, by Leonard Koren and Peter Goodman. Amazon.com price: $7.95 plus S&H.

Full Price: Competing on Value in the New Economy, by Thomas J. Winninger. Amazon.com price: $17.50 plus S&H.

RECOMMENDED READING LIST FOR SALES PROFESSIONALS

Your First Year in Sales, by Tim Connor. Amazon.com price: $19.95 plus S&H. Visit *www.timconnor.com.*

Exceptional Customer Service, by Lisa Ford, David McNair, and Bill Perry. Cost: $12.95 plus S&H, or visit *www.lisaford.com.*

The 12 Best Questions to Ask Customers, by Jim Meisenheimer. Cost: $19.95. Fax your order to 847-680-7881, or visit *www.meisenheimer.com.*

Telephone Tips that Sell, by Art Sobczak. Cost: $14.95 plus $3.50 S&H. 800-326-7721. Visit *www.businessbyphone.com.*

Integrity Selling, by Ron Willingham. Amazon.com price: $9.56 plus S&H.

GENERAL BUSINESS BOOKS

Growing Your Business, by Mark LeBlanc. Cost: $7.95 plus S&H. 800-690-0810. Visit *www.markleblanc.com.*

Swim With Sharks without Being Eaten Alive, by Harvey MacKay. Cost: $11.20 plus S&H at Amazon.com.

Taking the High Road: How to Succeed Ethically When Others Bend the Rules, by Frank Bucaro. Cost: $12.95 plus S&H at Amazon.com. Visit *www.frankbucaro.com.*

1001 Ways to Reward Employees, by Bob Nelson. Cost: $8.76 plus S&H at Amazon.com.

Complete Business Etiquette Handbook, by Marjorie Brody. Cost: $29.95. Visit *www.brodycommunications.com.* Phone 800-726-7936.

ABOUT THE AUTHOR

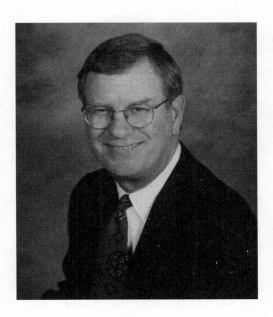

Bill Lee is the president of Lee Resources, Inc., a consulting and training firm that works with owners and general managers who want to enhance organizational productivity and with salespeople who want to increase sales and improve their gross margin.

Since 1989, as a speaker, trainer, and consultant, Bill has worked with more than 300 companies and with more than 30,000 owners, general managers, and salespeople to grow their business and improve profitability.

After graduating from Emory University in Atlanta, Bill joined New York-based GAF Corporation, where he became the youngest sales manager in that company's history. In 1969, Bill became a part owner in the start-up organization, Builder Marts of America, Inc. (BMA). By 1986, Bill's last full year with BMA, he and his partners had grown BMA from a start-up to over $640 million in sales.

In 1987, Bill sold his interest in BMA and founded Lee Resources, Inc.

In 1993, Bill earned the designation CSP (Certified Speaking Professional) from the National Speakers Association. He is also a charter member of Master Speakers International.

Bill's national clients include: Ace Hardware, Amaroc, American Wholesale, Andersen Window Corp., BMA, BMC-West, Budget Car Rental, Carolina Holdings, Datastream Corp., Do-It Best Corp., Drake Group, Lanoga Corp., Lumbermen's Merchandising Corp., National Gypsum Co., National Lumber and Building Material Dealers Association, Nextel, Owens Corning Fiberglas, Talk America, True Value Hardware, and Zep Manufacturing.

Bill can be reached at 800-808-0534 or at *billlee@mygrossmargin.com.*

This book is available at special quantity discounts to use as premiums and sales promotions, or for use in corporate training programs. For more information, please call the Special Sales Manager at 800-808-0534, write to New Oxford Publishing Corporation, P.O. Box 5558, Greenville, SC 29606, send a fax to 509-267-9711, or send an e-mail to *sales@mygrossmargin.com*.

For Additional Copies

To obtain additional copies of this book, photocopy or remove this form and mail or fax the completed form to the address below. Or call, fax, or e-mail us with your information. (Inquire about quantity discounts for your entire sales staff.) Bookstore, dealer, or distributor inquiries are welcome.

Please send me _____ copies of *Gross Margin: 26 Factors Affecting Your Bottom Line* @ $29.95 (+ $3.50 shipping U.S., $7 foreign, U.S. funds).

Name:_____

Company: _____

Address:_____

City:_____State_____ Zip_____

Phone_____Fax_____

E-mail_____

_____ Check here if you would like to receive Bill's ezine newsletter, published every two weeks.

Method of Payment

_____Visa _____MasterCard _____AMEX _____Discover

#_____

Signature_____

_____ Check or money order enclosed

Ways to Order
By phone: 800-808-0534. By fax: 509-267-9711. By mail: Gross Margin, P.O. Box 5558, Greenville, SC 29606. Or via e-mail: *sales@mygrossmargin.com.*

To order a copy of the "26 Factors" poster mentioned on page 5, phone 800-808-0534, send an e-mail to *poster@mygrossmargin.com,* or send a check to P.O. Box 5558, Greenville, SC 29606. Cost: $4.95 plus $2.75 S&H.